A PRACTICAL GUIDE TO DECODING YOUR

DREAMS & VISIONS

OTHER BOOKS BY ADAM THOMPSON AND ADRIAN BEALE

The Divinity Code to Understanding Your Dreams and Visions

BOOKS BY ADAM THOMPSON

The Supernatural Man

From Heaven to Earth

BOOKS BY ADRIAN BEALE

The Lost Kingdom

The Mystic Awakening

A PRACTICAL GUIDE TO DECODING YOUR

DREAMS & VISIONS

UNLOCKING WHAT GOD IS SAYING
WHILE YOU SLEEP

ADRIAN BEALE & ADAM F. THOMPSON

DESTINY IMAGE® PUBLISHERS, INC.

P.O. Box 310, Shippensburg, PA 17257-0310

"Promoting Inspired Lives."

This book and all other Destiny Image and Destiny Image Fiction books are available at Christian bookstores and distributors worldwide.

Cover design by Eileen Rockwell

Interior design by Terry Clifton

For more information on foreign distributors, call 717-532-3040.

Or reach us on the Internet: www.destinyimage.com

ISBN 13 TP: 978-0-7684-1230-7

ISBN 13 EBook: 978-0-7684-1231-4

For Worldwide Distribution, Printed in the U.S.A.

1 2 3 4 5 6 / 20 19 18 17

CONTENTS

SESSION ONE   Dreams and Visions and Controversy 7

SESSION TWO   First Things First 27

SESSION THREE   The Purposes of Dreams and Visions. 39

SESSION FOUR   Are All Dreams from God? 53

SESSION FIVE   Activating Dreams and Visions. 73

SESSION SIX   Counterfeit Interpretations 87

SESSION SEVEN   Beyond Dreams and Visions 99

SESSION EIGHT   The Language of Dreams. 123

     Answer Key. 151

     About the Authors 155

DREAMS AND VISIONS AND CONTROVERSY

Welcome to this exciting, informative, and interactive course on how to interpret dreams and visions. You will discover that the realm of dreams and visions is much broader than you may have realized. With this understanding, Scripture will open to you like never before.

Using our popular book, *The Divinity Code to Understanding Your Dreams and Visions,* as a basis, this guide explores the depths of how the Lord speaks to you and His unwavering desire to communicate with you. We urge you to thoughtfully consider each of the lessons and take time to listen to God's still, small voice speaking to your spirit—in familiar and perhaps unfamiliar ways.

If you hold preconceived notions about the nature of dreams and visions, we ask that you put those on hold while we together examine what the Word of God has to say about the subject. It is important to allow God to have His will and way in our lives—and sometimes that means opening our hearts and minds to the dreams and visions He shares with us.

Throughout the guide are pertinent questions and points to ponder, as well as a review at the end of each session to reinforce what you have learned. As an expansion of *The Divinity Code to Understanding Your Dreams and Visions,* this guide is designed to engage you in the work of the Holy Spirit as He brings you into a new realm of spiritual awareness—to bring you closer to the God who speaks to you in dreams and visions.

Cited within the following pages are many instances of biblical characters experiencing visions and God-induced dreams—as well as modern-day, personal encounters with God through visions and dreams. The authors share dramatic dreams and exciting experiences to confirm the relevancy of such occurrences in today's chaotic world—making sense out of much that might otherwise be confusing.

GREAT CONTROVERSY

The subject of dreams and dream interpretation is one of great controversy within the Body of Christ. Some believers fear that if we open ourselves to this method of guidance from God, it will put us in a position to be easily misled and sidetracked away from the fundamental teachings of the Bible. However, the opposite is true.

The Church must be totally soaked in the Scriptures if it is going to embrace the Holy Spirit's voice through dreams. It takes a balanced view of the whole of Scripture to interpret dreams and visions correctly; therefore, people who want to improve their interpretation skills have to be disciplined in Bible reading. They also have to believe and apply what they read.

Rather than being led astray, embracing dreams as messages from God actually leads us deeper into the ways of God. This is because, through dreams, the Holy Spirit teaches the application of the principle of referencing (or linking truth with truth), as detailed in the Scriptures: *"...the Holy Spirit teaches, comparing spiritual things with spiritual"* (1 Cor. 2:13).

THE DEVIL'S DOING

The real basis of this controversy is the devil's doing. The devil wants to prevent the empowerment of God's people through this channel of communication. He constantly attempts to thwart the purposes of God. Listen to his voice through Peter as Jesus begins to reveal spiritual truth incomprehensible to the natural mind:

> *From that time Jesus began to show to His disciples that He must go to Jerusalem, and suffer many things from the elders and chief priests and scribes, and be killed, and be raised the third day. Then Peter took Him aside and began to rebuke Him, saying, "Far be it from You, Lord; this shall not happen to You!" But He turned and said to Peter, "Get behind Me, satan! You are an offense to Me, for you are not mindful of the things of God, but the things of men"* (Matthew 16:21-23).

Just as the devil used Peter's personal agenda and limited outlook to challenge Christ, he is still using those whose security is not truly in God to stifle God's plans. If we have our security in anything other than Christ alone—position, money, power, recognition, religion, intellect, or

8

acceptance—the old self will come out fighting as soon as a spiritual truth threatens that security, *"for the flesh lusts against the Spirit...and these are contrary to one another..."* (Gal. 5:17).

SEE VISIONS AND DREAM DREAMS

On the day of Pentecost, Peter aligned the outpouring of the Holy Spirit in Jerusalem with an earlier prophecy made by Joel the prophet (see Joel 2:28-32):

> *And it shall come to pass in the last days, says God, that I will pour out of My Spirit on all flesh; your sons and your daughters shall prophesy, your young men shall see visions, your old men shall dream dreams* (Acts 2:17; cf. Joel 2:28).

Many believers realize that today's days are the last days, yet oftentimes Christians struggle with the idea of dreams and visions being from God—and for us today. The reality is that God is speaking to humankind as a whole and desiring for all of us to awaken spiritually and tune in to what He is saying by His Spirit.

Some today are like the Pharisees of Jesus' day—claiming to have a relationship with Jesus yet ignoring the Holy Spirit, just as they ignored Jesus. Many don't deny what God did in the Bible but struggle with what He is doing *today*.

LIVE BY FAITH

Others opt out of the spotlight of what God wants to do in this generation by choosing to live in the past or the future. It is an amazing thing that we can believe for yesterday and we can believe for tomorrow, but we struggle with faith for today—and yet that is what faith is: *"Now faith is the substance of things hoped for, the evidence of things not seen"* (Heb. 11:1). And further, it is meant to be our everyday experience: *"...The just shall live by faith"* (Rom. 1:17).

However, we do not like to live by faith. We would much prefer to have our security in something material. Consequently, we have become like Gideon, looking at past events recorded in the Bible and accepting what happened in those times (see Judg. 6:13). But in order for that to not interfere with our reality today, we deal with it by putting it into some dispensational phase of what God was doing "back then."

Approximately what percentage of your daily life do you *"live by faith"*? One-hundred percent? Seventy-five percent? Fifty percent? Less than twenty-five percent? Explain.

_____

_____

_____

_____

_____

_____

_____

_____

_____

On the other hand, we are also like Pharaoh, who, when asked, "When do you want God to move?" said, "How about tomorrow?" (see Exod. 8:9-10). By distancing ourselves in this way, we deny that we have ignored the Spirit of God, and we also pacify our consciences with the fact that some day in the future God will again move in power. For the most part, we don't deny God did what He did in the Bible—we struggle with what He is doing today.

Some modern-day churches are not even aware that God speaks through dreams and don't realize the importance of dreams in the plans and purposes of God. Too many have forgotten that the promise of the Holy Spirit brings with it God's prophetic guidance through dreams and visions.

Unfortunately, many Christians look at dreams, visions, and interpretations as the equivalent of Nebuchadnezzar's magicians and remain skeptical. Many have thrown the baby out with the bathwater when God is calling for an army of Spirit-intuitive Daniels to arise!

How open are people in your fellowship to hearing God's voice through dreams and visions?

_____

_____

_____

_____

_____

_____

Why do you think this is the case?

Human beings know instinctively that God is a miracle-working God, which is confirmed throughout the Bible. The Bible also says that God has not changed (see Mal. 3:6) and that He is the same today as He has ever been (see Heb. 13:8). But the truth we really need to take to heart is that *He is still the miracle-working God for those who have ears to hear* (see Matt. 13:9).

HEARING GOD'S VOICE

Are we missing truth from the Spirit of God by discrediting our dreams as not from God? If so, we are shutting ourselves off from hearing God's voice through dreams and are becoming hardened against it; as a consequence, "*...the wicked one comes and snatches away what was sown in* [our hearts]" (Matt. 13:19). A simple test is this: Can you remember the last three dreams you had?

Proponents of the New Age movement and some schools of psychoanalysis have embraced dreams in their hunger for answers to life's questions. However, being without the Holy Spirit, who is the Author (see Acts 2:17) and Interpreter (see Gen. 40:8) of dreams, they are in the dark—blind leaders of the blind.

Hear now My words: If there is a prophet among you, I, the Lord, make Myself known to him in a vision; I speak to him in a dream. Not so with My servant Moses; he is faithful in all My house. I speak with him face to face, even plainly, and not in dark sayings... (Numbers 12:6-8).

In these verses from Numbers 12, God is making a point to Aaron and Miriam, who were complaining about Moses. In vindicating Moses, God shows exactly how prophets other than Moses received their revelation. He says it comes to them in the *dark sayings of a dream or vision.* The word here for "dark sayings" is the Hebrew word *chidah,* which literally means "a puzzle, riddle, or parable." That God likes to communicate using parables is further displayed in His Word through Hosea, when He says:

I have also spoken to [you through] the prophets, and I gave [them] many visions [to make My will known] and through the prophets I gave parables [to appeal to your sense of right and wrong] (Hosea 12:10 AMP).

IMPORTANCE OF PARABLES

Not only did God speak to the prophets in the Old Testament using parables, but He also spoke through the prophets by having them act out His Word using parable-type messages. The following are three examples:

- Hosea married a harlot to show Israel's unfaithfulness to God (see Hos. 1:2).

- Ezekiel had to dig through a wall in the sight of the house of Israel to convey that they would go into captivity (see Ezek. 12:5).

- Jeremiah was to break an earthen flask in the sight of the elders of Jerusalem to show how God was going to break Jerusalem (see Jer. 19:10-13).

Later, we find in the Gospels that Jesus Himself used more than fifty parables to teach the truths of the Kingdom of God. In fact, parables were His preferred teaching method! Should it be a surprise to us that God is still using parables today?

God uses our personal parables to speak His truth in a way that we can relate to. Has He spoken to you in this way?

_____

_____

_____

_____

_____

_____

_____

If you think God is speaking to you in a parable dream but are unsure:

* Ask yourself, "Have I seen this before?"

* Consider, "Is there a biblical precedent?"

* Search for Scriptures relating to the words or images in your dream.

Dream interpretation resources are available, but they should be secondary to the Bible. Remember that interpretation is not a "formula" but rather is more "fluid" in nature. When we receive revelation and understand what God is saying, we can see Heaven manifest on earth.

List three parables and where each is found in the Scriptures:

_____

_____

_____

_____

_____

_____

_____

_____

_____

Write your favorite parable in your own words using a modern-day situation or circumstance.

_____

_____

_____

_____

_____

_____

_____

_____

_____

_____

_____

HOLY SPIRIT-EMPOWERED

The Holy Spirit empowered Joseph, Jacob's son, to interpret Pharaoh's dreams: *"And Pharaoh said to his servants, 'Can we find such a one as this, a man in whom is the Spirit of God?'"* (Gen. 41:38). And the Holy Spirit, acknowledged by Nebuchadnezzar, gave Daniel the incredible insight he possessed.

> *Belteshazzar [Daniel], chief of the magicians, because I know that the Spirit of the Holy God is in you, and no secret troubles you, explain to me the visions of my dream that I have seen, and its interpretation* (Daniel 4:9).

These verses illustrate that there are layers in the Scriptures to which we are not always sensitive. If we learn to hear the voice of God in the realm of dreams and visions, Scripture will open to us in new and exciting ways.

Joseph and Daniel were especially endowed with the Spirit of God. They were men God positioned specifically at the right place and at the right time to be used through dreams, visions, and the interpretation thereof. God is pouring out the same Spirit of which Joseph and Daniel were partakers, but in greater measure (see John 14:12), on you and me today!

Therefore, if we are going to be used of God to the measure He has planned, we need to recognize that our dreams are deeply significant in the plan of God for our lives. Like He did with Daniel and Joseph, God, through dreams, is speaking and preparing us for what He has brought us forth to accomplish at this time.

There is a mission for you and me that will not be fully realized unless we move on the instruction we receive through dreams. Likewise, if we are going to understand what God is saying to us in these dream messages, we need to repent of our insensitivity to the Holy Spirit and cultivate a relationship with Him.

Do you have reason to repent of your inattentiveness to the Holy Spirit's nightly nudging?

How intent are you on cultivating a relationship with the Holy Spirit?

Within Scripture are encoded, deeper truths.

Joshua and Caleb entered the Promised Land and represent a new generation not bound to Egypt (the world) in their thinking. Joshua was *"a man in whom is the Spirit"* (Num. 27:18). And Caleb, the Bible records, *"has a different spirit in him"* (Num. 14:24). Who did *not* enter the Promised Land? Those who did not believe God after He had brought them out of Egypt, those who continued to see things only in the natural (see Num. 13:33).

There is a generation of people who know the Word of God, who are born again, and who see God's Kingdom on the pages of the Bible but fail to enter into what God has for them because they are prepared only to think naturally, or rather, are not prepared to think spiritually (see Isa. 55:8-9; Rom. 8:5-6).

Now we know this is not you, or you would not have chosen to study the subject of God's dreams and visions through this manual. However, there is a group of people in danger of dying in the spiritual training ground that is designed to teach them Kingdom dynamics (see Deut. 8:2-3) unless they are prepared to be led by the Spirit of God into the Promised Land in the next phase of their journey. These are people still holding on to past tradition and religious practices. If we deny His leading, we will remain spiritual babes, regardless of our Bible knowledge or title within the church (see Rom. 8:14; Heb. 6:1).

How have you prepared yourself to listen to God?

When has He spoken the loudest to you? The softest?

God can speak however you are prepared to listen.

God can speak through the *rhema* word and through visions. Dreams and visions are two of the ways we receive the spoken word or message from God. Their main purpose is to create, build, and strengthen faith. As the sword of the Spirit, dreams and visions also divide between soul and spirit, joints and marrow, and are used by the Holy Spirit to disclose the thoughts and intents of the heart and to confirm direction.

So then faith comes by hearing, and hearing by the word of God (Romans 10:17).

The *"word of God"* in this Scripture is the Greek word *rhema*, which is the enlightened, spoken word of God. It can also refer to immediate utterances from the Holy Spirit.

But He answered and said, "It is written, 'Man shall not live by bread alone, but by every word that proceeds from the mouth of God'" (Matthew 4:4).

God also speaks through songs, nature, and numbers. Perhaps you awaken with a song on your mind. This can be the Lord speaking to you. Think through the words of the song. Encoded in that song may be a message that God is trying to convey to you.

Or maybe you feel closest to God when you are walking through a park, in the woods, or sitting along the shoreline of a lake or ocean. Nature, God's creation, can bring a special peace to hearts, souls, and minds when you allow yourself to drift into His presence.

> ### How does receiving a dream, vision, or revelation affect you?

We don't live in just this realm; we live in a spiritual realm beyond what we can see. Dreams and visions are insights into that realm. If the characters in the Bible had ignored the guidance they received through dreams, there would be:

- No Isaac (see Gen. 20:3,6-7)

- No Israel (see Gen. 41:37-41; 45:5; 50:20)

- No Solomon's kingdom (see 1 Kings 3:5-15)

- Less understanding of future world events (see Dan. 2; 4)

- No Jesus (see Matt. 1:20-24; 2:13,22)

Now, if there had been no Jesus, there would be no salvation through His death upon the cross. If there had been no salvation, there would be no release of the Holy Spirit. If there is no means of salvation and no release of the Holy Spirit, humankind is without eternal life and we are forever doomed to be permanently separated from the presence of God.

UNBELIEVERS AND VISIONS

What about unbelievers who receive visions? Unbelievers who receive visions do so through occult means, such as drugs and divination. Drug use opens people up to the spirit realm of demonic deception. In fact, when you dig beneath the English translation of the Scriptures to the original languages, you discover that drug use is directly linked to witchcraft. The word "sorceries" in Revelation 9:21 is the Greek word *pharmakeia*. This is the word from which we get the word "pharmacy." *Pharmakeia* is translated as "witchcraft" in Paul's list of works of the flesh given to the Galatian church (see Gal. 5:20).

The Bible reveals that people operating under the influence of familiar spirits are empowered to see in the spirit realm. This is evident when Paul and Silas are thrown into prison for casting out a spirit of divination from a fortune-telling slave girl in the Book of Acts:

> *Now it happened, as we went to prayer, that a certain slave girl possessed with a spirit of divination met us, who brought her masters much profit by fortune-telling. This girl followed Paul and us, and cried out, saying, "These men are the servants of the Most High God, who proclaim to us the way of salvation." And this she did for many days. But Paul, greatly annoyed, turned and said to the spirit, "I command you in the name of Jesus Christ to come out of her." And he came out that very hour (Acts 16:16-18).*

After Paul had commanded the spirit to come out, the Scripture says:

> *But when her masters saw that their hope of profit was gone, they seized Paul and Silas and dragged them into the marketplace to the authorities (Acts 16:19).*

It is pretty obvious that it was the spirit within the slave girl that gave her the ability to see in the spirit realm, and once he was removed, she was no longer able to receive her spiritual visions. This explanation adequately accounts for the reaction of the slave girl's masters, whose hope for further profit was taken away when the spirit was cast out of her.

SLEEP IS AS DEATH

In Scripture, sleep is as death. Take the example of the death of Lazarus:

> *These things He [Jesus] said, and after that He said to them, "Our friend Lazarus sleeps, but I go that I may wake him up." Then His disciples said, "Lord, if he sleeps he will get well." However, Jesus spoke of his death, but they thought that He was speaking*

about taking rest in sleep. Then Jesus said to them plainly, "Lazarus is dead" (John 11:11-14).

Paul used the metaphor of sleep too:

For anyone who eats and drinks [without solemn reverence and heartfelt gratitude for the sacrifice of Christ], eats and drinks a judgment on himself if he does not recognize the body [of Christ]. That [careless and unworthy participation] is the reason why many among you are weak and sick, and a number sleep [in death] (1 Corinthians 11:29-30 AMP).

David wrote of it in the Psalms as well:

Consider and hear me, O Lord my God; enlighten my eyes, lest I sleep the sleep of death (Psalm 13:3).

Death is a separation of the body and spirit; sleep allows your spirit to be freed up to accept dreams and communications from God. When we sleep, we have the capacity to move into the spiritual realm where God can communicate to us through dreams and visions.

A Dream Is a Word from God

Joseph received dreams from the Lord, but they took time to be fulfilled:

Until the time that his word came to pass, the word of the Lord tested him (Psalm 105:19).

What was the Lord testing, or growing, in Joseph during the time between when he received his destiny dream and when it actually came to pass?

This truth is confirmed by the prophet Daniel:

I thank You and praise You, O God of my fathers; You have given me wisdom and might, and have now made known to me what we asked of You, for You have made known to us the king's [word] (Daniel 2:23).

In Hebrew, the word used for "word" is מִלָּה, *millah*, which means "dream, matter, word, or thing."

That very hour the word [millah] was fulfilled concerning Nebuchadnezzar; he was driven from men and ate grass like oxen; his body was wet with the dew of heaven till his hair had grown like eagles' feathers and his nails like birds' claws (Daniel 4:33).

In each of these references, a dream from God is considered to be a word from God. It is a *rhema* word from God that gives the dreamer faith, strengthens them, and has an application for their life.

God speaks to us in whatever way we are willing to listen. Everyday occurrences become supernatural when they are touched by the revelation of God. Broaden your mind-set to understand that God can speak to you in a number of ways.

SUMMARY

* Hold off on making a judgment about dreams and visions until you've heard what the Bible has to say on the matter.

* We are standing in the last days, which are marked by an outpouring of God's Spirit.

* The outpouring of the Spirit includes prophecy through dreams and visions.

* The Holy Spirit is the current representative of the Godhead on earth today.

* We can have a propensity to live in the past or in the future to avoid exercising faith today.

* The call to live by faith is a call to hear what God is saying today.

* As Christians, we are prone to "throw the baby out with the bathwater" because we see the New Age movement and psychoanalysis embrace dream interpretation for guidance.

* Old Testament prophets heard God's Word, as we do, through parable-type dreams and visions.

- Jesus' preferred teaching method was to use parables.

- Christian leaders, because of their busyness, can expect God to speak to them in their downtime (sleep) through dreams and visions.

- We will miss the current outpouring of the Spirit if we don't have ears to hear.

- Dreams are for both the Christian and non-Christian; visions, on the other hand, are the domain of the believer.

PRAYER

Father, I believe You still speak to people. I am thankful and humbled that You desire to speak to me. As I step into this journey, Lord, I pray that You will open my spirit to hear what You are saying to me. I pray for an open heart to hear You in new and exciting ways. In Jesus' name, amen!

SESSION ONE REVIEW

1. ☐ TRUE or ☐ FALSE: God speaks to His people in only one way—through Scripture.

2. God used Moses' staff to divide the Red Sea. What else has the ability to divide?
   A. Visions and dreams
   B. An angry reply
   C. The sword of the Spirit
   D. All of the above

3. How many parables did Jesus use when He was teaching about the Kingdom of God?
   A. Twelve
   B. More than fifty
   C. Seventy times seven
   D. Less than fifty

4. ☐ TRUE or ☐ FALSE: There are layers in the Scriptures to which we are not always sensitive.

5. Which of the following are ways God speaks to people, other than Scripture?
   A. Visions and dreams
   B. Nature
   C. Numbers and songs
   D. All of the above

6. In Scripture, sleep is often a metaphor for _____.
   A. death
   B. hypocrisy
   C. condemnation
   D. miracles

7. What is the *rhema* word?

    A. Scripture enlightened for immediate application

    B. A word from God that strengthens you and gives you faith

    C. The Holy Spirit illuminating truth for you

    D. All of the above

8. ☐ TRUE or ☐ FALSE: There is no biblical precedent for the idea that a dream is a word from God.

9. ☐ TRUE or ☐ FALSE: God wants to use you as a vehicle to bring the revelation of Heaven into a manifestation on earth.

10. Explain the significance of the Hebrew word *chidah* and how it relates (or doesn't relate) to "dark sayings."

_____

_____

_____

_____

_____

_____

_____

_____

_____

Personal Application

It should now be clear that God speaks to us in whatever way we are prepared to listen. In the following sessions, you will learn how to hear God in new and wonderful ways. At the same time, though, it is important to realize that each person is created with unique receptors to relate to God. It is beneficial to be aware of our individual design so that we can use it to tune in to the voice of God.

Look through the following list of some of the common ways that people most easily hear God. Think through each one and circle the two or three options that best describe you. If there is a way you are "prepared to listen" to God that is not listed, add it to the list.

- *Worship.* Singing, playing an instrument, or being in a worship service helps you feel close to God. Perhaps God uses songs to speak to your spirit.

- *Intellect.* You hear God best when you study the Scripture. Perhaps digging into concordances, apologetics, or in-depth sermons helps open your ears to God's voice.

- *Supernatural Activity.* Dreams, visions, prophetic words, signs, and wonders are some of the best ways for you to hear God.

- *Community.* Being with God's people energizes and refreshes you. You see God's activity in their lives and can hear God's voice clearly through healthy relationships.

- *Nature.* God speaks to you when you are in His creation.

- *Service.* Through volunteering at church, serving the poor, and "doing" the work of the Gospel, you feel that you are in a place where you can hear the Holy Spirit speak.

- *Quietness.* You prefer to seek God in solitude and hear Him in the quiet moments you spend alone with Him.

Reading and Response

Read *Genesis chapters 37, 40, and 41.*

Then read the Foreword and Chapter 1 as well as pages 145-155 of *The Divinity Code to Understanding Your Dreams and Visions* by Adam Thompson and Adrian Beale.

Write in your own words what the Bible has to say about dreams and visions.

_____

_____

_____

_____

_____

_____

_____

_____

_____

_____

_____

_____

_____

_____

_____

_____

_____

_____

_____

_____

FIRST THINGS FIRST

Before proceeding in your study of dreams and visions, it is important to take time to address some of the common mistakes people make. The first is skipping the instructions in a book like *The Divinity Code* and heading straight to the metaphor dictionary in the back of the book. At best, this headlong dive into dream interpretation can result in frustration and, at worst, open the door to dangerous theology.

> *For the word of God is living and powerful, and sharper than any two-edged sword, piercing even to the division of soul and spirit, and of joints and marrow, and is a discerner of the thoughts and intents of the heart* (Hebrews 4:12).

The Bible must always be the first reference for dreams and visions. The hidden truth the Bible reveals is that dreams have the power to divide between soul and spirit because they are a deposit of God's living Word to us today! To some, that is a very radical thought. You may be wondering, *Are you suggesting we should endorse extra-biblical revelation?* No! God is still speaking, and He didn't cease speaking at the completion of the canonical books of the Bible. The Book of Acts is an open-ended book, and it is still being written today. However, what God says today has to be in line with what He has said in the past (see Heb. 13:8). This is why the metaphors in *The Divinity Code* are based first and foremost on Scripture.

Let's use Joseph, briefly mentioned in the previous chapter, as an example. When Joseph was seventeen years of age, he dreamed two dreams that declared his brothers and his parents would someday bow down to him (see Gen. 37:5-11). His prideful boasting of this revelation, together with his father's favoritism toward him, put him at odds with his brothers, who then sold him to passing merchants. Consequently, Joseph's dreams lay dormant as he served as a slave and prisoner in Egypt.

Joseph was eventually used to interpret two of Pharaoh's dreams, which revealed that the nation of Egypt would experience seven years of abundance followed by seven years of severe famine (see Gen. 41:17-31). When Pharaoh heard Joseph's interpretation and his advice on how to handle the forthcoming blight, he appointed Joseph as the nation's prime minister. And yes, his brothers came to Egypt to buy food and found themselves bowing down unknowingly to their brother, just as had been foretold in Joseph's original dreams some twenty years prior. This remarkable story is recorded in the Book of Psalms:

> *Moreover He [God] called for a famine in the land; He destroyed all the provision of bread. He sent a man before them—Joseph—who was sold as a slave. They hurt his feet with fetters, he was laid in irons. Until the time that his [Joseph's] word came to pass, the word of the Lord tested him (Psalm 105:16-19).*

Notice that it says that Joseph was kept in prison *"until the time that his word came to pass"* (Ps. 105:19). Joseph's word was the dream he had received as a seventeen-year-old boy. Joseph's dream was God's word for him!

Often we are too close to the scene of the dream to really understand what it means. Dreams are part of God's ongoing Word to us. They are not the whole picture, but they accompany and augment what God is saying to us through His written Word and through prayer.

> *Then Joseph said to Pharaoh, "The dreams of Pharaoh are one; God has shown Pharaoh what He is about to do" (Genesis 41:25).*

> *We both had dreams," they answered, "but there is no one to interpret them." Then Joseph said to them, "Do not interpretations belong to God? Tell me your dreams" (Genesis 40:8 NIV).*

If interpretations belong to God, how can humans interpret dreams?

_____

_____

_____

_____

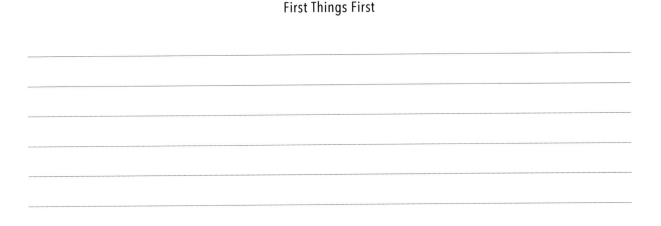

Correct interpretations come from knowing and trusting God intimately. He is the Source of both the dream and the interpretation, and He allows the Holy Spirit to share the dream's meaning with believers who are totally committed to Him.

COMMON MISTAKES

Treating dreams too casually and treating interpretation as a formula are common mistakes made by dreamers. Heading straight to the dream symbols dictionary in a book reveals a mindset of interpretation as a formula.

The following are types of things that must be taken into consideration when looking for an interpretation to any word from God, whether it be a prophecy, a vision, a dream, a word of knowledge, or a personal revelation:

- What else is going on in the verse or the scene?

- What other things is the dreamer experiencing?

- Where do these things occur in Scripture?

Not considering the context of dreams is another mistake. How do we find accurate context? A good starting place is to ask questions like:

- Who had the dream?

- When did they have the dream?

- What was in the dream?

- How did they feel when they had the dream?

- Where were they when they had the dream?

Dreams divide between soul and spirit, not just in the individual, but also at the family, church, business, national, and Kingdom levels. Often, what people think a dream means and what it turns out to signify can be radically different. Functioning like Nathan's parable to David (see 2 Sam. 12:1-13), dreams and their correct interpretations bypass the heart's natural defense mechanisms and allow the Holy Spirit to bring conviction and correction.

The following is a great example of how a properly contextualized dream can help discern and disclose hearts. One morning during a discussion with a group of people, a young man asked what it would mean if, in a dream, he had his hand on his ex-partner's throat. I asked him about the context of the dream and whether he had ever threatened her. He said that to his knowledge, he had never openly threatened her, though he admitted that she might feel threatened by him.

He also explained that the night before, he heard someone preaching and the sermon touched on forgiveness. He explained that before he went to bed, he had verbally forgiven his ex-partner. After probing the Scripture, the following verse illuminated the dream's interpretation:

> *But that servant went out and found one of his fellow servants who owed him a hundred denarii; and he laid hands on him and took him by the throat, saying, "Pay me what you owe!"* (Matthew 18:28).

The context of this verse is unforgiveness; I knew instantly what God was saying. As the essence of what God was saying was shared with the young man, the Holy Spirit powerfully witnessed to him and brought conviction. He was blown away that God, through a dream, was able to pinpoint the true state of his heart. Through the dream, God was showing him that he had not really forgiven his ex-partner—that in his heart he still held her responsible and was expecting an apology from her.

This is not only a great example of God's ability to divide hearts through dreams, but it also emphasizes the importance of using the Bible to find the correct interpretation of a dream. This method is especially useful if your metaphor dictionary does not have an entry that seems to fit the context of a particular dream.

DREAMS TEACH

In Matthew 5-7, Jesus delivers what is called the Sermon on the Mount. In the midst of this passage is a well-known verse that was cited previously but is worth quoting again: *"But seek first the kingdom of God and His righteousness, and all these things shall be added to you"* (Matt. 6:33).

This verse speaks about getting things right in our hearts and allowing God to rule and reign there, and it promises that if we do so, God will provide for our needs. This is a challenging verse, particularly when the world and external circumstances can be yelling for us to seek security everywhere else but in God.

Being human, it is "natural" to find comfort and security in the world. Being a spiritual being, do you find "supernatural" comfort and security in God?

_____

_____

_____

_____

_____

_____

_____

_____

_____

_____

Dreams have a capacity to teach at a number of levels. The majority of dreams are metaphors, parables, and riddles.

> *Jesus answered, "Very truly I tell you, no one can enter the kingdom of God unless they are born of water and the Spirit"* (John 3:5 NIV).

This experience that Jesus mentions reinforces a truth that Israel was meant to learn before they entered the Promised Land and that all of us, likewise, have to learn before we are able to move fully into the Kingdom. As Jesus, quoting Moses, puts it, *"Man shall not live by bread alone, but by every word that proceeds from the mouth of God"* (Matt. 4:4).

In fact, entering the Kingdom is dependent on this truth. Notice that this Scripture says that it is by every word that *"proceeds"* and not "proceeded." One is present tense; the other is past tense. We cannot move into the spiritual promises of God on yesterday's manna. We need a living Word today. Of course, the devil wants to shut this down because dreams have the capacity to provide a major component of what God is saying to us today. He knows that once this truth is out, the Church is once again on the move and closer to the Book of Acts!

SIMPLE DREAMS

Don't disregard a dream as the result of nighttime snacking simply because it doesn't have a lengthy storyline. Even the shortest dreams can speak revelation to us.

For example, when Jacob was fleeing because of death threats from his brother, Esau, he had an encounter with God at Bethel:

> *Then he dreamed, and behold, a ladder was set up on the earth, and its top reached to heaven; and there the angels of God were ascending and descending on it. And behold, the Lord stood above it, and said: "I am the Lord God of Abraham your father, and the God of Isaac; the land on which you lie I will give to you and your descendants. Also your descendants shall be as the dust of the earth; you shall spread abroad to the west and the east, to the north and the south; and in you and in your seed all the families of the earth shall be blessed. Behold, I am with you and will keep you wherever you go, and will bring you back to this land; for I will not leave you until I have done what I have spoken to you"* (Genesis 28:12-15).

What a fantastic encouragement this dream must have been to the anxious traveler, Jacob, heading to an unfamiliar destination. When God is rounding off this encounter with Jacob, He promises that He will not leave him until He has completed what He has *"spoken to"* him. To put it another way, He says that He will not leave him until He has completed *"His word"* to him. And what was His word to Jacob? It was the dream he had just been given.

This word so impacted Jacob that the Bible says, *"Then Jacob lifted up his feet, and came to the land of the people of the East."* (Gen. 29:1 KJV). The heaviness he had been experiencing was completely stripped from him because he had a word from God. He didn't think, *I shouldn't have eaten that pizza last night.* No, he recognized God's word when it came to him in a dream!

What are three common mistakes people make regarding dreams?

_____

_____

_____

_____

_____

God uses the elements of your day to speak to you through dreams and visions.

Summary

- A detailed study of the life of Joseph reveals that dreams are part of God's living Word. They augment what He is saying to us through the written Word and prayer.

- Jesus taught principles from a dream Solomon had 950 years earlier (see 1 Kings 3:5,9-13).

- According to a contextual understanding of Psalm 105:17-19, Joseph was refined through the dreams of Pharaoh's butler and baker. These dreams refined him while he waited for the word of his own dreams to be fulfilled.

- Dreams and their correct interpretation bypass the heart's natural defense mechanisms and allow the Holy Spirit to bring conviction and correction.

- Dreams have the power to divide between soul and spirit and disclose the thoughts and intents of the heart.

- The Kingdom of God is gained by receiving the ongoing _"word that proceeds from the mouth of God"_ (Matt. 4:4). Dreams are a major component of that ongoing Word.

- There is a need to repent and apologize to the Holy Spirit for our insensitivity toward and ignorance of His voice to us in the night.

Prayer

Father, You are both the Giver and the Interpreter of dreams. I give You my sleeping and my waking and invite You into my dreams. I pray for Your wisdom as I step into this journey of dream interpretation. Help me to avoid foolish mistakes and to hear Your voice clearly. Make me a priest who faithfully reveals Jesus to the world.

SESSION TWO REVIEW

1. ☐ TRUE or ☐ FALSE: When you have a dream that you would like to know the meaning of, your first course of action should be to consult a dream metaphor dictionary.

2. ☐ TRUE or ☐ FALSE: When you have a dream that you would like to know the meaning of, your first course of action should be to ask God what He is saying.

3. What is key to interpreting any word of God?

    A. Context

    B. A metaphor dictionary

    C. The gift of prophecy

    D. Training in dreams and interpretations

4. Which of the following questions would help establish the context of a dream?

    A. Who had the dream?

    B. Where and when did the dream occur?

    C. How did it make the dreamer feel?

    D. All of the above

5. What are common mistakes people make regarding dream interpretation?

    A. Not considering the dream's context

    B. Not taking a dream seriously

    C. Consulting a dream dictionary first

    D. All of the above

6. ☐ TRUE or ☐ FALSE: The majority of dreams are metaphors, parables, and riddles.

7. ☐ TRUE or ☐ FALSE: As a general rule, short dreams don't usually contain enough content to be significant.

8. Which of the following is a main door through which the enemy gains access into our lives?

    A. Trauma

    B. Abuse

    C. Unforgiveness

    D. All of the above

9. What are the first three steps one should take to accurately interpret a dream?

_____

_____

_____

_____

_____

_____

_____

_____

_____

_____

_____

_____

_____

_____

_____

_____

Personal Application

Read *Matthew 18*.

Unforgiveness can cause more damage to a human soul than almost anything else. It can damage relationships and cause anxiety, and it has been linked to physical illnesses like cancer. Unforgiveness can also cause tormenting dreams.

Spend some time alone with the Lord this week and ask Him to reveal any areas of unforgiveness in your heart. Sit quietly. If a person comes to your mind, think through any reason you may have unresolved anger or hurt toward that person. Ask yourself, *If I could, would I want this person to know he or she has hurt me? If I could, would I want an apology from this person?* An answer of "yes" to either of these questions is a good indicator of unforgiveness in your heart.

Ask the Lord for forgiveness for harboring unforgiveness. Make a choice to forgive those who have hurt you. Ask for help in forgiving them the way you have been forgiven in Christ Jesus.

Memorize *Luke 10:19*.

Reading and Response

Read Chapter 2 as well as pages 156-165 of *The Divinity Code to Understanding Your Dreams and Visions* by Adam Thompson and Adrian Beale.

What several considerations need to come first regarding dreams, visions, and the interpretation thereof?

Dream Notes

THE PURPOSES OF DREAMS AND VISIONS

As mentioned previously, *dreams and visions* are two of the ways we receive a spoken word or message from God meant to *create, build, and strengthen faith*. Session Three focuses on the many purposes of dreams and visions including *revelation, disclosure, warning, instruction, prophecy, and, of course, salvation*.

The story of Gideon (see Judg. 6-8) provides a good example of how a dream can *strengthen faith*. In this passage of Scripture, the story is told of how God visited and encouraged a man who was a self-designated weakling (see Judg. 6:15) to take on and defeat an innumerable Midianite army.

CREATING AND BUILDING FAITH

God had progressively built faith in Gideon through a series of confirming events. The final tool used to make the fearful Gideon resolute in faith was a dream! It was not a dream that Gideon had; rather, it was a dream that one of the enemy soldiers had, and Gideon heard it being told. Scripture describes the final scene before Gideon leads his carefully selected army against Israel's opponents as follows:

And when Gideon had come, there was a man telling a dream to his companion. He said, "I have had a dream: To my surprise, a loaf of barley bread tumbled into the camp of Midian; it came to a tent and struck it so that it fell and overturned, and the tent collapsed." Then his companion answered and said, "This is nothing else but the sword of Gideon the son of Joash, a man of Israel! Into his hand God has delivered Midian and the whole camp" (Judges 7:13-14).

The sudden barley loaf tumbling into the camp of Midian is a classic example of how metaphors are used in dreams today. Compared to wheat, barley is an inferior grain; its head contains fewer grains, it is more susceptible to loss through windstorms, and it is not as hard. The dream begins with the words, *"To my surprise a loaf of barley bread tumbled into the camp..."* (Judg. 7:13). Gideon was encouraged—he had his faith strengthened—by hearing a message from God given through a dream shared between two enemy soldiers.

Have you had your faith strengthened in an unexpected manner?

How can you intentionally build your faith in God?

REVELATION

There was a time in Israel's history when King Saul was looking for guidance because a large Philistine army was parked on his doorstep. Unfortunately, Saul had stumbled greatly in his walk with God because of his jealousy of David. Samuel, the nation's prophet, was dead, so Saul approached God in trepidation. The Scripture says, *"And when Saul inquired of the Lord, the Lord did not answer him, either by dreams or by Urim or by the prophets"* (1 Sam. 28:6).

Though Saul did not receive the revelation he was looking for in this situation, it is evident from Scripture that God regularly used dreams to answer questions (see Dan. 2:29). He continues to use the same method today.

Have you allowed unforgiveness or a haughty attitude to break your direct lifeline to God?

Is there something or someone obstructing communication between you and God your Father?

In *The Divinity Code* is the tale of a modern-day dream with a Scripture that instantly came to the interpreter's spirit:

> *For you know that afterward, when he wanted to inherit the blessing, he was rejected, for he found no place for repentance, though he sought it diligently with tears* (Hebrews 12:17).

After explaining the dream, the interpreter pleaded earnestly that the person concerned would understand the gravity of the situation. This was a sobering reminder that God is both a God of love and also a consuming fire (see Heb. 12:29).

Not many of us appreciate correction. The Bible captures this truth well when it says:

> *Now no chastening seems to be joyful for the present, but painful; nevertheless, afterward it yields the peaceable fruit of righteousness to those who have been trained by it* (Hebrews 12:11).

By the grace of God we are saved through the death of His dear Son Jesus Christ (see Eph. 2:8-9). Therefore, when a dream shows an area that needs change, it is important that the people concerned understand that it is God's trifold goodness that is bringing this area into the spotlight.

Has the good Lord brought to your attention a rotten apple in your life that needs to be done away with? Have you dealt with it?

_____

_____

_____

_____

_____

_____

_____

_____

_____

How gracefully do you accept warranted chastisement when God or someone in your life presents it to you?

_____

_____

_____

_____

_____

_____

_____

_____

_____

_____

_____

God cares enough about His children individually that He doesn't want any of us to get hurt. At these times, the call upon us is to trust Him, for He sees beyond the moment and knows what awaits us around the corner. As a God of love, He is always moving with our best interests at heart.

PROPHECY

Nothing strengthens faith like a prophetic word. For this reason, the Word of God, through dreams, is often loaded with promises for the future. Operating in this way, a dream brings Heaven to earth in an instant and opens new frontiers and opportunities not thought of by the dreamer. Through prophetic dreams, God is able to encourage, prepare, marshal, and direct His troops for the expansion of the Kingdom.

Nothing strengthens faith like a prophetic word.

It is the same today as it was in the dream revealed to Gideon (see Judg. 7:13-14), in the promise to Jacob (see Gen. 28:12-15), and in the dreams of Pharaoh (see Gen. 41:1-7). Through a prophetic dream, God may open His ministers to be led more by the Spirit, as the following dream shows:

I saw a river running diagonally through what was currently the church congregation's sitting area. It ran between the pulpit and the congregation. At the back of the church were huge stands—like in a football stadium. When I awoke, I was concerned because I thought that the river separated the speaker from the audience.

I believe the river in this dream represents the flow of the Holy Spirit. The fact that the river flowed in front of the speaker is a good thing as it means that the preacher is putting the Spirit before himself. When this is done, God will draw crowds of people—hence the stands. The dreamer's concern about the river in front of the speaker indicates that moving in the Spirit is not something they are comfortable with at this stage and that God is challenging them in this area.

Through a prophetic promise given in a dream, God may also remind those with the call of God on their lives that the gifts and callings of God are irrevocable—they are under full warranty and are never canceled or rescinded (see Rom. 11:29).

Are you aware of—have you discovered—your God-given gifts and callings?

Are you using your gifts and callings for God's glory?

DISCLOSURE

Dreams may foretell things that are going to happen tomorrow, or they may foretell something that is going to happen twenty years from now. It is not always possible to clearly define the timeline in which God is operating. For this reason, it is wise not to follow Joseph's example (see Gen. 37:5-7) and to avoid sharing everything revealed with everyone. It is better to be like Mary, who *"...kept all these things and pondered them in her heart"* (Luke 2:19).

When Israel was about to go to battle, God told them that they were to separate from their ranks those who were fearful—those without faith for the situation (see Deut. 20:8). God had them remove the spirit of fear because it has an incredible ability to be transferred. In the same way, Jesus removed the doubters when He was about to resurrect Jairus' daughter from the dead (see Matt. 9:18-26).

Similarly, it is wise to be very selective about the people to whom you reveal what God is promising you. Not everyone knows or appreciates the call of God on your life, and if you share or surround yourself with people who are not able to see you in the Spirit, their doubt may undermine your faith and begin a decay of the promise within you (see 2 Cor. 5:16).

> Do you surround yourself with positive supporters who encourage you or negative naysayers who spread fear and doubt about almost everything?

SALVATION

Indeed God speaks once, or twice, yet no one notices it. In a dream, a vision of the night, when sound sleep falls on men, while they slumber in their beds, then He opens the ears of men, and seals their instruction, that He may turn man aside from his conduct, and keep man from pride; He keeps back his soul from the pit, and his life from passing over into Sheol (Job 33:14-18 NASB).

God speaks to the unsaved at least twice through dreams during their lifetime to get them saved, so passionate is He that they spend eternity with Him. He has made provision through His own death upon the cross that no one need go to hell. The passage from Job 33 reveals that unbelievers don't understand what they have received in their dreams due to the veil upon their hearts. They desperately need someone with the Spirit of God to enlighten them.

In the same way, God wants to release the prisoners of satan today and bring them into God's courts. Everyone who does not know Christ—rich or poor, educated or untaught, successful or unsuccessful, whether they realize it or not—is a slave of satan. Stop and think about that for a while; it puts things back into perspective. This truth is outlined by Paul in his instructions to Timothy:

In meekness instructing those that oppose themselves; if God peradventure will give them repentance to the acknowledging of the truth; and that they may recover themselves out of the snare of the devil, who are taken captive by him at his will (2 Timothy 2:25-26 KJV).

These verses not only point out, as highlighted, that the people of the world are satan's captives, but they also say that people of the world *"oppose themselves."* This is because in resisting the Gospel, people are not so much opposing the Church or the Gospel but are in fact keeping themselves bound under satan's jurisdiction and are therefore really opposing themselves. They want to experience freedom, but in its place they have captivity!

Regularly, friends ask about dreams that unsaved people they know have been having—like the nurse whose patient repeatedly dreamed of compulsive cleaning, the father who continually dreamed of falling, the young man who often dreamed of struggling to get the manhole hatch in the ceiling open, or the lady who repeatedly saw herself running down a hallway to get away from the fire that was chasing her.

All of these dreams are God speaking to these people about their need for salvation. Dreams and their interpretations are an untapped reservoir of opportunities. If we lift our eyes and learn to interpret dreams, then there is truly a white harvest field of souls before us (see John 4:35).

Have you experienced an unsettling recurring dream?

Have you considered it an important enough dream to try and interpret it?

SUMMARY

- Dreams and visions are *rhema* words from God to build and strengthen faith.

- Like Gideon, who was strengthened in faith by hearing two enemy soldiers sharing a dream, you can be strengthened in faith by hearing the dreams of others.

- Dreams and visions reveal secrets and answer questions that are on people's hearts.

- Dreams are a powerful vehicle for God to warn and guide His people. This is particularly true for those who are embarking on new journeys with God, because the enemy is constant in his endeavors to abort the promises of God.

- Dreams are used to correct, as is shown in the Book of Job, where God uses dreams to turn people from their dastardly deeds.

- The prophetic nature of many dreams strengthens faith and endurance.

- It is not wise to disclose every dream or vision you receive because many people will not appreciate or understand the call of God upon your life. Your listener's doubt is like fear, which may begin a decay of the promise of God within you.

- Dreams are a regular means by which God communicates to non-Christians their need for salvation.

- Everyone who has not come to the cross of Christ is a prisoner of satan.

- According to Job, God is so passionate about people's souls that He uses dreams at least twice during their lifetime to prevent them from going to hell.

- Everyone dreams; therefore, skills developed in dream interpretation create new harvest field opportunities.

PRAYER

Father, I recognize that You speak to me in my dreams. Even when my body is asleep, my spirit is awake, ready to receive from You. I ask for my heart to be primed and ready to hear what You are speaking to me in the night watches. I pray for ears to hear and a heart to understand what You have to say to me about my life, my family, my church, and my community. I pray for warning, rebuke, encouragement, new revelation, and messages of love from You. Speak, Lord, Your servant is listening. In Jesus' name, amen!

SESSION THREE REVIEW

1. ☐ TRUE or ☐ FALSE: One of the purposes of visions and dreams is fortune-telling.

2. What is the purpose of visions and dreams?
   A. Salvation
   B. Building faith
   C. Revelation
   D. All of the above

3. Through prophetic dreams God can _____.
   A. scare people
   B. encourage and prepare believers
   C. direct His faithful followers
   D. B and C

4. ☐ TRUE or ☐ FALSE: The Word of God, through dreams, is often filled with His promises for the future.

5. ☐ TRUE or ☐ FALSE: The emotions we feel in a dream are important in determining the context of a dream.

6. ☐ TRUE or ☐ FALSE: When you have a dream, your first response should be to use a dream metaphor dictionary to look up the objects in your dream.

7. A dream brings Heaven to earth _____.
   A. in an instant
   B. to open new opportunities
   C. to expand the Kingdom
   D. all of the above

8. How is Joseph a picture of Jesus?
   A. He was hated by his brethren

    B.   He was sold for silver

    C.   He was falsely accused

    D.   All of the above

9.   According to Second Timothy 2:25-26, who holds people captive?

    A.   The devil

    B.   Themselves

    C.   Pastors

    D.   A and B

10. Explain why God is so merciful that He offers all people many opportunities to accept His salvation—even through their dreams.

_____

_____

_____

_____

_____

_____

_____

_____

_____

_____

_____

Personal Application

You now know that there can be many layers of meaning and application in Scripture. As you read your Bible this week, be deliberate about how you read. Read slowly. Ask the Holy Spirit to open your eyes to what He wants to reveal to you through the Scripture. Note that there may be a literal, immediate application for the people in the story, an application for Israel or the Church, and/or an application for you. Try this method by reading Genesis 24.

Memorize *Acts 2:17*.

Reading and Response

Read Chapter 3 as well as pages 165-175 of *The Divinity Code to Understanding Your Dreams and Visions* by Adam Thompson and Adrian Beale.

What do you consider to be the two most important purposes of dreams and visions? Explain.

DREAM NOTES

ARE ALL DREAMS FROM GOD?

Are all dreams from God?

Before you proceed, candidly answer this question with the knowledge you have right now.

_____

_____

_____

_____

_____

_____

_____

_____

_____

_____

Because of the nature of some dreams, many people think that God is not the author of all dreams. We believe that God speaks to us through every dream, but is He the author of every dream? Yes and no. The vast majority of our dreams are God speaking directly to us. However, the Scriptures also seem to indicate that the enemy has an ability to provide visionary experiences, and we ourselves are able to influence what God reveals through our dreams.

You may be thinking, *What if I have a nightmare? Is that from God? Or if I have a demonic attack in my dream, is that from God?* The truth is, as Christians, even when we are awake, the enemy is looking for opportunities to attack us and bring us down.

Session Four is an in-depth exploration of this topic. *The Divinity Code* is even more comprehensive and will, no doubt, answer all your questions regarding who is the originator of your dreams.

WHILE SLEEPING

While we are sleeping, our spiritual senses can pick up spiritual warfare or demonic oppression (in the heavenlies) that may be occurring in the area. It is important to remember that Jesus has defeated the enemy (see Col. 2:15). The Bible also declares that we have been given the authority to trample on snakes and scorpions and power over all the capabilities of the evil one (see Luke 10:19). Praise God!

Consider the enemy for a moment. When Jesus was led by the Spirit into the wilderness to be tempted by the devil, the devil was able to manifest a vision. The Bible records, *"Then the devil, taking Him up on a high mountain, showed Him all the kingdoms of the world in a moment of time"* (Luke 4:5).

Note that the devil was able in some way to provide a vision of the world's kingdoms. Who led Jesus into this situation to be tempted? God—the Spirit—did (see Luke 4:1). God was always in control. He knew the enemy's abilities and allowed it. Who authored the vision? On one level, the devil did; but on a far superior level, God did because He had foreknowledge of the devil's plan, permitted it, and used it in accordance with His will and purpose.

Were you surprised to read that the devil authored the vision Jesus saw? Is this an unsettling realization? How do you feel about God allowing Jesus to be tempted?

_____

_____

_____

_____

_____

_____

_____

_____

_____

_____

We must always remember that the enemy can do only what God permits. For this reason, we should not be too quick to ignore or discredit any dream on the grounds that "it is not from God."

NIGHTMARES

Primarily, a nightmare is a signal—the cry of a heart carrying an unresolved issue that needs attention. Generally, if Christians are walking in the Spirit and living in the counsel of the Lord, they do not have nightmares. However, if, as a Christian, you have constant nightmares, there is definitely a heart issue to be resolved.

Some prophetic dreams and visions may come across as nightmares because of the enormity of the events shown in them. These are normally received by people with a strong prophetic calling. For example, Daniel experienced this type of nightmare while lying on his bed (see Dan. 4:5).

Constant nightmares probably mean that there is an oppression operating in your life. This may indicate that you are being harassed by an oppressing spirit. Oppression is not possession but rather harassment. This occurs when there is a stronghold in your mind or heart due to something that has happened in the past that has affected you deeply, such as an abuse or trauma of some kind. If this is the case, you will require some counseling and ministry of the Holy Spirit under the guidance of a discerning and trusted mature believer. Ultimately, what we look for in these situations is the legal ground on which the enemy is allowed to gain access. Legal ground in this context refers to an action, word, or deed contrary to the written Word of God. For this reason it is important for believers to know and understand their rights as sons and daughters in the New Covenant.

The enemy can gain access when we sin with our mouths—when we curse ourselves or others by labeling ourselves or others as "idiots," "fools," etc. This can also happen if we make negative confessions, such as, "I must be going crazy." Similarly, we may be guilty of openly confessing doubt or fear, which gives the enemy the right to harass and torment us. Cursing ourselves and denying the Word of God grieves the Holy Spirit and gives a foothold to the enemy (see Eph. 4:27-30). We need to be ever aware that *"…we do not wrestle against flesh and blood, but against principalities, against powers…in the heavenly places"* (Eph. 6:12).

How closely do you guard your words? Do you think before you speak all of the time, most of the time, some of the time, or never?

As Christians, we must be very careful what we say and confess with our mouths. The Book of Proverbs says *we have power in our tongues to speak words of life or death* (see Prov. 18:21). This is not an empty platitude that we can choose to ignore; this is a living reality that we need to take to heart. Therefore, it is vitally important always to speak as if we are speaking the very words of God and to have our vocabulary consistently lined up with the Word of God—this empowers us to receive the promises of God.

When we align our speech with God's Word in this way, we frustrate the enemy because God's Word cannot be broken (see John 10:35). Jesus tells us, *"Heaven and earth will pass away, but My words will by no means pass away"* (Matt. 24:35).

TEMPTATION

It is evident from Scripture that God allows the enemy access to us to test or to prove us. Although He was without sin, Jesus was tempted by the devil in the wilderness (see Luke 4:1-13). This temptation may come in the form of a dream or a vision, as it did with Christ. As previously shared, Luke's Gospel records, *"Then the devil, taking Him up on a high mountain, showed Him all the kingdoms of the world in a moment of time"* (Luke 4:5). The fact that the devil was able to show Jesus all the kingdoms of the world *"in a moment of time"* suggests that this temptation came in the form of a vision.

Why would God allow the enemy to tempt us? The answer to that question is twofold. If we fail the test, it acts like a refining fire by bringing what is truly in our hearts to the surface so that we deal with it. It thus produces a humbler and holier disciple.

Do you more often pass or fail the tests that God sends your way?

_____

_____

_____

_____

_____

_____

_____

God also allows us to undergo temptation so that when we have come through the temptation victoriously, we are aware that we have grown stronger in God and have moved to another spiritual level. For Christ, graduation through His wilderness temptations meant that He was now ready for ministry.

> *Then Jesus returned in the power of the Spirit to Galilee, and news of Him went out through all the surrounding region. And He taught in their synagogues, being glorified by all* (Luke 4:14-15).

Job's Example

Reading the Book of Job, we find that he was a righteous man. There was no one like him on the earth, and he was righteous to the point where God proclaimed his righteousness. The devil came to God, and God asked him where he had been, to which he answered, *"From going to and fro on the earth..."* (Job 1:7). He was looking to find legal ground to enter the lives of men and women on earth, particularly those who were in relationship with God, which at the time included Job. That didn't just happen to Job without reason.

This passage of Scripture shows us what can potentially happen to all saints. In the spirit realm, there is a constant battle going on, and the enemy is on the prowl, looking to devour believers and constantly accusing them before God (see 1 Pet. 5:8).

Has God allowed a catastrophe in your life and then rewarded you for being faithful to Him?

_____

_____

_____

_____

_____

_____

_____

_____

_____

_____

_____

_____

_____

Then satan went out from God's presence to bring calamity to Job. The encouraging thing in the Book of Job is that all the hardship and all the attacks of the enemy purged him and caused him to be stronger, wiser, and more faithful to the Lord, even though at one point he seemed to be weak in his faith.

Job was not suffering because of sin, but God in His foresight knew that in suffering Job would sin. It was God's wisdom at work, because He hadn't finished with Job. God wanted him to come to the fullness He had for him. This attack on Job's life included nightmares. Job himself said, _"Then You scare me with dreams, and terrify me with visions"_ (Job 7:14).

Job attributed the nightmares to God. It appears he experienced them because God allowed the devil access to him. God took down the hedge of protection around Job (see Job 1:10), a spiritual hedge that we likewise are protected by if we are born again and living rightly before God (see Ps. 34:7; Isa. 5:1-2).

Have you ever felt the absence of God's hedge of protection from around your life?

_____

_____

_____

_____

_____

_____

_____

_____

_____

If yes, how and when did it return?

_____

_____

_____

_____

_____

_____

_____

_____

_____

Job's protection was removed for his benefit and for ours—so we could see what happens in the spirit realm. Today, God doesn't freely give evil spirits access to our lives without them having some legal right to that access. These situations happen if there are unresolved issues that give the enemy legal ground to come into God's Kingdom—that is, you (see Luke 17:21).

Common grounds on which the enemy gains access:

* Unforgiveness related to some form of abuse or trauma (see Matt. 18:21-35)

* Rebellion and unrepentant sin (see Prov. 17:11)

* Witchcraft and divination (see 1 Sam. 15:23; 16:14)

* Generational curses (see Exod. 20:4-5; Deut. 5:9)

* Wrong confession with our mouths (see Eph. 4:25-27)

* Extreme jealousy, envy, or rage (see Eph. 4:25-27)

* Strongholds: defiant mental attitudes contrary to the Word of God (see 1 Sam. 15:23; Prov. 17:11)

How many times have you allowed the enemy to gain access into your life via one or more of these doorways?

_____

_____

_____

_____

_____

_____

_____

_____

_____

Do you have one or more open doors today that need to be closed? What is holding you back?

_____

_____

_____

_____

_____

_____

_____

_____

_____

_____

If you are experiencing pornographic dreams, there is generally a core issue, as outlined above—often having more than one strand and manifesting itself as lust. The devil has been known to build a stronghold of lust around a threefold cord of jealousy, unforgiveness, and mental strongholds. There can also be a spirit of perversion operating in the lives of pornographic nightmare sufferers. This means that when dealing with this problem, it is necessary to address more than just the manifesting problem of lust.

The pornographic nightmare sufferer needs to come clean with heart issues through confession and repentance so that the enemy has no legal ground for entry. Then a prayer identifying and severing spiritual bonds or soul ties should be declared in authority over the believer. It is important that this problem is not further fed by the dreamer by looking at other people with lust, because that gives the enemy further ground on which to enter. Like Job, all believers need to make a covenant with their eyes when thoughts stray beyond pure relationships, particularly when battling with lust (see Job 31:1).

PARABLES IN DREAMS

God communicates to us using parables in dreams to bring us His wisdom. Just as Jesus spoke in parables, talking about seed sowing to the farmer (see Matt. 13:3-9), about fishing to fishermen (see Matt. 4:19), and about finance to stewards (see Matt. 25:14-30), so He speaks to us in allegorical dreams today. It's clear that God speaks to us in riddle-like dreams, and we need the Holy Spirit to give us the spiritual insight to interpret these parables and riddles.

When Jesus explained a particular parable by saying that what comes out of the mouth comes directly from the heart, Peter came up to Him and petitioned, *"Explain this parable to us."* Jesus said in response, *"Are you also still without understanding?"* (Matt. 15:15-16). Even though he was awake and in the physical presence of Jesus, it is obvious that Peter still didn't understand the parable and needed to have it explained or interpreted for him. Likewise, we experience parable-type communication from God through our dreams and also need it interpreted if we are going to understand it.

Jesus relates to all people at their level and on their wavelength through everyday realities and experiences.

When we stop and think about it, Jesus Christ is the best Communicator the world has ever known because He relates to all people at their level and on their wavelength through everyday realities and experiences. He did it when He was physically here on earth, and He is still doing it through our dreams by His Spirit while He is with the Father.

WHY METAPHORS?

God uses metaphors because images are very powerful. God created our minds to relate to and remember images and sounds more quickly and more readily than written words. For example, on most computer desktops there is a trash can for deleted files. When you delete something on your computer, do you look for the words "trash can," or do you look for the little image of the trash can? Everybody responds to the icon more quickly than the words.

Are you a "visual" learner? How easy is it for you to envision the scenes in the Bible?

This is because, although our verbal thoughts can be very fast, visual images received by our brains are much faster. Compared to visual processing, trying to take in information by reading is much slower. When we read, we have to comprehend it. We read it first and then have to create the image in our minds. On the other hand, seeing an image or hearing a sound has the potential to go straight into our minds and our spirits.

This is why the Internet, television, radio, and other such media are very influential forms of communication. The Internet is powerful because it is full of images and can be used for good—and for evil. I am not saying the Internet is wrong; it is an effective means of communication and a great source of information. Unfortunately, this information highway is also being used to flood and corrode our society with a plethora of pornographic, occult, and other ungodly information and images.

Hungry for Answers

God also uses parables because He knows that we will be hungry to discover what our dreams mean. As soon as we understand that God speaks to us this way, we get even hungrier to know what He is saying. As the Scripture says, *"It is the glory of God to conceal a thing: but the honour of kings is to search out a matter"* (Prov. 25:2 KJV).

> Would you rather take matters as they are and be satisfied, or are you more likely to knock on His door, ask the Expert, and search for His answers?

_____

_____

_____

_____

_____

_____

_____

_____

_____

_____

It is inherent in us to search for the answer to the code—the divinity code—He has set before us. Indeed, there is a blessing for those with this hunger, because the Bible declares that there is fulfillment in asking, seeking, and knocking (see Matt. 7:7).

So God speaks to us in parables because they relate to us and have a greater potential to be anchored in our minds, just as Jesus' disciples remembered His teachings and, later, wrote the Gospels. He also encodes His wisdom using metaphors because they are more readily received, they create a hunger in us for the interpretation, and they bypass our heart's natural self-protective tendencies.

BIASED DREAMS

God may reveal the agendas in our hearts through our dreams. This seems to be the essence of God's communication through Jeremiah:

For thus says the Lord of hosts, the God of Israel: Do not let your prophets and your diviners who are in your midst deceive you, nor listen to your dreams which you cause to be dreamed (Jeremiah 29:8).

It may be that this verse refers to a "self-generated" dream, or that it may equally be explained by another Scripture:

Therefore speak to them and tell them, 'This is what the Sovereign Lord says: When any of the Israelites set up idols in their hearts and put a wicked stumbling block before their faces and then go to a prophet, I the Lord will answer them Myself in keeping with their great idolatry (Ezekiel 14:4 NIV).

This says that if we come to God with preconceived plans (our idols), then God will answer us (in this case, in a dream) according to that which is in our hearts. God causes the dreamer to dream a dream that reveals the idolatry within his or her heart. In terms of God's statement to Jeremiah, these are the dreams *"you cause to be dreamed"* (Jer. 29:8). The dream is a message from God to show dreamers the state of their hearts and is designed to bring them back to God.

TAKE DREAMS SERIOUSLY

Finally, if we believe that God is the author of only some dreams, and if we dismiss the weird ones as either from the enemy or figments of our own imagination, we have become like those who rule out unpalatable passages of Scripture as uninspired. *I like that dream, but I don't like that one.* So all the nice dreams are from God, and all the others—the corrective and disciplinary ones—are from the enemy.

When we pick and choose which dreams are inspired and which are not, we close ourselves off from the full counsel of God. The ultimate consequence of this is spiritual insensitivity, leading to an imbalanced and powerless Christian walk.

Is it uncomfortable to deal with, or even think about, real heart issues?

Are all dreams from God?

Does your answer to the previous question differ from the one you gave at the beginning of the session?

Rather than ignoring them, we are to realize that dreams are dealing with real heart issues. Consider how much of the problem of our heart's insensitivity or bias is addressed when we begin to see that God is communicating through all dreams and start to take them all seriously.

SUMMARY

- God can speak through every dream.

- Some prophetic dreams come across as nightmares because of the enormity of the events they portray.

- Constant nightmares point to an oppression operating in the life of the dreamer.

- Negative confession may give the enemy ground on which to harass us.

- It is important to have our vocabulary line up with the Word of God.

- Our victory over principalities and powers comes from being in harmony with God's Word.

- God allows demonic harassment so that we learn to overcome through the blood of the Lamb and the word of our testimony.

- We are particularly susceptible to temptation in our dreams. These moments refine or approve us.

- The Book of Job provides insight into the spirit realm. The devil is constantly seeking permission to enter the lives of people. He cannot do anything without legal ground, which he presents to God to gain access.

- Common grounds on which the enemy gains access include:
  - Unforgiveness
  - Rebellion
  - Witchcraft
  - Generational curses
  - Wrong confession
  - Extreme jealousy, envy, and rage
  - Mental strongholds

- Pornographic nightmares may indicate a multi-stranded stronghold, which manifests and operates as lust.

- Spirit-sensitive counseling is suggested for nightmare and pornographic dream sufferers.

- God uses adversity to refine us.

- Dreams may appear weird because God uses parables to communicate to us.

- Jesus is the best Communicator the world has ever known because He employs parables using everyday realities to speak to every person at his or her own individual level and wavelength.

- God uses metaphors because:
  - They create a more memorable message.
  - They are more readily heard.
  - They stimulate reflection and action.
  - They readily convey vision.
  - They refocus the familiar in a new light.
  - They bypass the heart's self-protective mechanisms.

- God speaks through every dream.

- God, the devil, and our own hearts influence the dreams we dream.

- Beware of idols in your heart because God will answer you according to your idols.

- Be slow to discredit dreams on the basis of their apparent source.

- Don't pick and choose which dreams you think are inspired.

- Take all dreams seriously.

PRAYER

Father, You are unlocking new levels of revelation in my life, new depths of understanding in the spirit realm. I pray for a spirit of understanding as I learn the ministry of dream interpretation. I pray for divine opportunities to minister truth to those to whom You are speaking through dreams and visions. I ask for an anointing to pinpoint exactly what it is You are saying in a dream and for a supernatural ability to communicate Your heart through the understanding of dreams. May I be a blessing to You and Your people. In Jesus' name, amen!

SESSION FOUR REVIEW

1. Are all dreams from God?
   A. Yes
   B. Yes and no
   C. No
   D. Maybe

2. What may be the cause(s) of constant nightmares?
   A. Oppression operating in the dreamer's life
   B. The devil's harassment
   C. Sinful self-talk
   D. All of the above

3. God does *not* allow us to undergo temptation to:
   A. Build our egos
   B. Grow stronger
   C. Advance spiritually
   D. Be victorious

4. ☐ TRUE or ☐ FALSE: The enemy constantly accuses believers before God and hopes to devour us.

5. If you have a dream about another person:
   A. God may be speaking to you about yourself through the character of that person.
   B. God may be using the role or position of that person to speak to you about your situation.
   C. The name of that person may have a meaning or message for you from God.
   D. All of the above

6. What is a common ground on which the enemy gains access?

    A. Forgiveness

    B. Unforgiveness

    C. Hospitality

    D. Generosity

7. ☐ TRUE or ☐ FALSE: Dreams about high-profile figures—e.g., actors, politicians, superheroes—should be disregarded as they probably have nothing to do with us.

8. ☐ TRUE or ☐ FALSE: There is no hope of recovery for sufferers of pornographic dreams or nightmares.

9. What is likely to happen if we pick and choose which dreams to take seriously?

    A. We will miss important messages from God.

    B. We will close ourselves off from the full counsel of God.

    C. We will become spiritually insensitive.

    D. All of the above.

10. Explain how if you have a dream about another person, that dream may not actually be about the other person but about you.

....

....

....

....

....

Personal Application

It's time to start dreaming. If you haven't already, begin to pray that the Lord would speak to you in your dreams. God will speak to you in the way you are prepared to listen. Take some deliberate steps to invite Holy Spirit activity into your dreams.

  ▪ At least one hour before going to bed, turn off your electronic devices. Don't check e-mail, watch the news, or scroll through social media. Don't even read books. Instead, begin to prepare your spirit to meet the Lord in the night watches.

* If you are in the habit of planning your next day's activities or worrying over tomorrow's to-do list right before you go to sleep, take time to plan the next day's schedule earlier in the evening. This will allow your mind to be free from the burden of planning or worrying.

* Place a notebook and pen near your bed.

* Arrange your evening schedule so you can have a quiet time with the Lord immediately before going to sleep.

* Right before going to sleep, engage your spirit and welcome the Holy Spirit. Put on worship music. Pray or sing in tongues. Worship. Read a passage of Scripture or meditate on a specific verse. Invite the Holy Spirit to speak to you in your dreams.

* When you wake in the morning, be cognizant of any dreams, impressions, songs, numbers, names, or words that are on your mind as you rise. Write these down in your notebook.

* Ask the Lord to reveal to you what He is speaking to you. Look for Scriptures regarding the elements of your dream. Consult *The Divinity Code* for help with any metaphors you may not understand.

Memorize *Psalm 127:2* in the version of your choice. The New American Standard Bible is especially beautiful as it indicates that God not only gives sleep to His beloved, but that He also ministers to His beloved even as they sleep. When your body is asleep, your spirit is awake, communing with the Father.

Reading and Response

Read Chapters 4 and 5 as well as pages 175-184 of *The Divinity Code to Understanding Your Dreams and Visions* by Adam Thompson and Adrian Beale.

What stood out to you the most as you read these two chapters?

ACTIVATING DREAMS AND VISIONS

...I will pour out My Spirit on all flesh; your sons and your daughters shall prophesy, your young men shall see visions, your old men shall dream dreams (Acts 2:17; Joel 2:28).

This passage in Acts 2 and Joel 2 reveals a link between prophecy and dreams and visions. In reality, dreams and visions are vehicles to bring us into the prophetic. That is not to say that we are all prophets in the fivefold ministry sense of the word (see Eph. 4:11). However, dreams and visions are primary ways in which God communicates to His prophets. This is confirmed when God says through Moses, *"...If there is a prophet among you, I, the Lord, make Myself known to him in a vision; I speak to him in a dream"* (Num. 12:6).

SENSITIVITY

A person might have the powerful spiritual gift of seeing in the Spirit as a seer (one who has visions), prophesying, or even interpreting dreams, but it is another thing to have the sensitivity of heart to know if, when, and how to deliver what is shown. The prophetic is as much about knowing what to do with what God shows you as it is about having the discernment of heart to receive what He shows you.

At times, God will simply give people spiritual insight so that they can pray for those to whom the revelation relates, often without those whom it concerns knowing it. We always need to ask the Holy Spirit for wisdom to match the gift, because although our hearts may be zealous, the Holy Spirit helps us to be effective.

Have you felt led to pray for someone close to you? A coworker? Someone you pass on the street? Have you responded to or ignored the inkling?

_____

_____

_____

_____

_____

In pouring out His Spirit, God has equipped all of us with the ability to prophesy. That should get us excited and expectant. Just as God told Israel to begin to possess the land inhabited by the enemy as they moved from the wilderness into the Promised Land, so God tells us to spiritually step into what He has for us today (see Deut. 2:24,31). As with Israel, God is encouraging us to begin possessing what belongs to us, because without the understanding that it is ours, we lack the faith to step into it.

God has equipped us all to prophesy.

Having been stirred to move in the spiritual gifts, such as prophecy, we need to understand that God doesn't just wave a wand and give us them overnight. It is a gradual process—and there will be times when we make mistakes. When I first started moving in the prophetic, I became discouraged if I made an error. I thought that perhaps I had misunderstood God and that He didn't really want me to move in the gifts. However, I have discovered that it doesn't matter if we make mistakes. The Lord will help us to grow while learning from our mistakes.

If given a prophetic word from God, would you share it immediately with the person whom it concerns?

_____

_____

If given a prophetic word from God, would you be afraid to share it for fear of making a mistake?

Getting visions is common among prophetic people and those who are baptized in the Holy Spirit and moving in spiritual gifts. A vision can come either while we are awake or while we are asleep. Often visions come and we are not even aware that we have received one. I personally have found that two of our most receptive times for receiving visions are just before we fall asleep or, conversely, just as we are stirring to consciousness but not yet awake. At these times, because of our insensitivity to the voice of the Spirit, we are prone to miss what God is saying, as *the person without the Spirit does not accept the things that come from the Spirit of God but considers them foolishness…"* (1 Cor. 2:14 NIV).

DEPOSIT FROM GOD

A vision is a revelation straight to the human spirit, a deposit from God conveyed directly to our spirits that interrupts soulish or conscious activity. However, without spiritual discernment, our natural inclination is to ignore such revelations as random thoughts of our own mind.

When you read the previous paragraph, did something stir within you? Have you, perhaps, been receiving downloads from God that you've dismissed?

I often get visions when I pray for people. It is very much like having a dream while being awake. These visions are mostly metaphorical or symbolic in nature. However, they can also be literal. When God gives me the interpretation of the vision, much like He would a dream, and I speak it out, it becomes a powerful prophecy in the lives of those for whom I am praying.

I remember once praying for a young man, and as I prayed, God gave me a vision of him working at a tire business. In the vision, he was working at a blue bench, and in front of him was a windowsill that had a potted plant on it. I saw him looking out the window, dreaming about the desires of his heart. As I described the scene, he told me that I had described his workplace with incredible detail. He said he actually did look out the window and daydream about the things he wanted. The vision and the prophecy that went with it encouraged him in the Lord by revealing that God cared about him individually and had a plan for his life.

How to Experience Visions

You may be wondering, *How can I experience visions?* Well, it is simple! Visions are just one of the ways God's Word is communicated to us when we earnestly desire to hear and fulfill His will. God uses visions from cover to cover of the Bible to communicate with humankind. He used a vision to speak to Abram: *"After these things the word of the Lord came to Abram in a vision..."* (Gen. 15:1). And He used visions when giving the apostle John the Book of Revelation: *"...I heard the number of them. And thus I saw the horses in the vision..."* (Rev. 9:16-17).

Beginning with Moses' words to Israel about the purpose of the wilderness wanderings, we read:

> *And you shall remember that the Lord your God led you all the way these forty years in the wilderness. ...So He humbled you, allowed you to hunger, and fed you with manna which you did not know nor did your fathers know, that He might make you know that man shall not live by bread alone; but man lives by every word that proceeds from the mouth of the Lord* (Deuteronomy 8:2-3).

Here God wants us to see the parallel between physical hunger and its spiritual counterpart. While not denying our physical need (*"man shall not live by bread alone"*), the emphasis is on understanding that our greatest need is spiritual food: *"...but man lives by every word that proceeds from the mouth of the Lord"* (Deut. 8:3).

Our greatest need is spiritual food.

How important is this? In case we miss it, as the Israelites did in the wilderness, Jesus comes to our rescue in the New Testament by restating these exact words when tempted by physical hunger (see Matt. 4:4; Luke 4:4). Jesus graduates and Israel fails because Jesus was hungrier for God's Word than for physical food! Our friend Job brings us this same truth when he says, *"...I have treasured the words of His mouth more than my necessary food"* (Job 23:12).

By allowing Jesus to complete the picture for us in John's Gospel (when speaking to His disciples about the Samaritan harvest), God links the fulfillment of His will with food. When Jesus' disciples requested that He eat, Jesus responded by saying, *"I have food to eat of which you do not know"* (John 4:32).

When you hunger to know God's Word and fulfill His will with similar fervency, you can be sure He will communicate to you, and one of His main methods will be visions.

On a scale from one to ten, how hungry are you to know God's Word and fulfill your God-given destiny?

_____

_____

_____

_____

_____

_____

_____

_____

FERVENT PRAYER

The Bible says that whatever we sow we will also reap (see Gal. 6:7). This is a universal truth. If you sow righteousness, you will reap righteousness. If you sow sin, you will reap sin. When it comes to sowing into prayer and having a passion to seek God for periods of time, you will reap the rewards. God has also promised that He is a rewarder of those who diligently seek Him (see Heb. 11:6).

What are you sowing for His glory and your purpose?

_____

_____

_____

_____

_____

_____

_____

What are you reaping for His glory and your purpose?

_____

_____

_____

_____

_____

_____

_____

_____

LED BY THE HOLY SPIRIT

There is nothing better in life than being led by the Holy Spirit.

Jesus knew the woman at the well had had five husbands, and it opened her up to receiving what Jesus was saying to her and led her to gather the townsfolk, which set the scene so that revival could break out (see John 4).

If we claim to know Jesus, the Bible says we will walk the way He walked (see 1 John 2:6). Jesus was the Prophet of all prophets. He did not need any promotion or publicity. The power of the Holy Spirit was His herald, drawing crowds through signs and wonders.

What does it mean to you to be led by the Holy Spirit?

_____

_____

_____

_____

_____

_____

_____

How different would your everyday walk through life be if you were being led by the Holy Spirit?

_____

_____

_____

_____

_____

_____

_____

Visions allow the Holy Spirit to prepare the ground, open people, and build faith for what will follow. Even now you may be receiving things in the Spirit, but not understanding them. God could be revealing to you the future plans of the enemy operating in the second heaven (the spiritual realm) so that you can prepare for spiritual warfare. Or He could be showing you the third heaven (where He dwells) and its storehouse of miracles. These spiritual downloads empower us to *call those things which do not exist as though they did* (see Rom. 4:17) and see them manifest in the natural realm.

WAIT UPON THE HOLY SPIRIT

When God doesn't immediately provide an interpretation for a dream or vision, it may be that He has a deeper revelation to bring to you (see John 11:6,25). It may also be that God is using the timing of the interpretation to develop patience (see James 1:3), create greater faith (see Heb. 11:9-10), or profoundly strengthen the inner self by causing us to wait upon God with greater desire (see Isa. 40:31).

Sometimes one dream or vision may not give enough of the message for it to be definitively interpreted. In this case, further revelations—in visions and dreams—will give direction to the interpretation.

Are you still waiting for the interpretation of a dream or vision you had?

Are you being patient and waiting on the Holy Spirit?

It is also possible that the delay between the revelation and its interpretation is designed to prevent human effort from sabotaging God's purpose. Whatever the reason, whenever we receive a dream or vision, we should always wait upon the Holy Spirit to provide the interpretation. However, if one is not immediately forthcoming, we can rest assured that God will always bring forth an answer in His time and with our best interests at heart.

SUMMARY

* According to Acts 2:17, dreams and visions bring us into the realm of the prophetic.

* We grow in the prophetic, learning from our mistakes.

* The prophetic is as much about knowing what to do with what God shows us as it is about having the discernment of heart to receive what He shows us.

* Two very receptive times for receiving visions are 1) when you are beginning to fall asleep and 2) when you are beginning to awaken.

* Metaphoric and literal elements can be combined in dreams and visions.

* A vision is one way God's Word is communicated to us when we earnestly desire to hear and fulfill His will.

* We are to hunger for God's Word and the fulfillment of His will more than we hunger for our natural sustenance.

* If we sow in prayer, we will reap His answers.

* Visions allow the Holy Spirit to prepare the ground, open people, and build faith for what follows.

* When an interpretation of a vision or dream is not immediately forthcoming, we can be sure that God will bring it in His perfect time and with our best interests at heart.

PRAYER

Father, thank You for the baptism in the Holy Spirit. Thank You for the baptism of fire. I pray for a fresh infilling of the Spirit. I pray for a fresh baptism into the Spirit. I want every gift that You are offering me. I want to speak in tongues; I want to prophesy; I want to operate in signs, wonders, and miracles. I ask for the full operation of all the revelatory gifts—dreams, visions, words of knowledge, and wisdom. I want to glorify Jesus through these beautiful gifts. I ask for them now with an expectant and grateful heart. In Jesus' name, amen!

SESSION FIVE REVIEW

1. ☐ TRUE or ☐ FALSE: In pouring out His Spirit, God has not equipped all of us with the ability to prophesy.

2. Dream and visions are primary ways God communicates with His _____.
    A. priests
    B. disciples
    C. prophets
    D. creatures

3. ☐ TRUE or ☐ FALSE: We may make mistakes when first moving in our spiritual gifts.

4. When given a powerful spiritual gift, we must be _____.
    A. eager to use it right away
    B. passive and apprehensive
    C. very cautious
    D. sensitive and discerning

5. When are the two of the most receptive times for receiving visions?
    A. Just before falling asleep and right before waking
    B. At midnight and 2 a.m.
    C. At dawn and dusk
    D. During daytime catnaps

6. ☐ TRUE or ☐ FALSE: A vision can come while you are awake or asleep.

7. A vision is a:
    A. Meandering of our minds
    B. Revelation straight to our spirits from God
    C. Soulish activity

    D.   Demonic apparition

8.   ☐ TRUE or ☐ FALSE: Jesus had visions.

9.   ☐ TRUE or ☐ FALSE: You cannot experience a vision.

10. Why does God speak in metaphors?

_____

_____

_____

_____

_____

_____

Personal Application

Read *Acts 10.*

Have you been filled with the Holy Spirit as described in Acts 2? If you are saved, you received a measure of the Holy Spirit when you gave your heart to Jesus. The baptism of the Holy Spirit is a separate event that fills us with the Holy Spirit and allows us to receive the fullness of His gifts. The evidence of being filled with the Spirit is the gift of tongues—a heavenly prayer language that is described in Romans 8:26-27. If you have not had this life-changing experience, Jesus wants to baptize you in the Holy Spirit! Begin to ask God to fill you with His Spirit.

> Identify times in your day when your hands are busy but your mind is not engaged. This is a great opportunity for you to exercise your spirit self and engage the Holy Spirit through speaking in tongues. It could be when you are driving to work, folding laundry, taking a shower, cutting the grass, etc. Use these moments to speak, pray, and sing in tongues! Your spirit self will be activated and you will be poised to hear more clearly from God.

Memorize *Luke 11:13.*

Reading and Response

Read Chapter 6 as well as pages 184-193 of *The Divinity Code to Understanding Your Dreams and Visions* by Adam Thompson and Adrian Beale.

Explain the difference between the manifestation of God and God Himself.

DREAM NOTES

COUNTERFEIT INTERPRETATIONS

It is God's will for us, through the Holy Spirit, to prophesy and to have dreams and visions. However, it is one thing to have dreams and visions. Where we go to obtain their interpretation is an entirely different matter. Many unknowingly turn to the occult in their desire for answers.

At this point, it is important to understand that the devil is *not* part of the Godhead. He is actually a fallen angel, a created being that cannot create anything but mayhem. While it is impossible for him to constructively create, he is the master of imitation and deception. As the thief, he attempts to use imitation to steal the glory that rightly belongs to God and to rob the inheritance that belongs to God's children—us (see John 10:10).

Have you or do you know people who have consulted the occult to help them make decisions or look into the future? Why is that wrong?

When we look at those who dabble in occult practices, such as tarot cards, astrology, palm reading (even interpreting dreams), we see the devil imitating and perverting what God has intended for the saints.

> Do you or someone you know read horoscopes every day in hopes of knowing what is going to happen? Why is that wrong?

_____

_____

_____

_____

_____

_____

_____

_____

Likewise, when people go to clairvoyants, they are visiting counterfeit prophets and seers. Clairvoyants have an inherent sensitivity to the spirit realm and most likely have ungodly spirits operating in their lives (see Acts 16:16; 1 Sam. 28:7). Having bought the devil's lie, clairvoyants enter the heavenlies illegally and assist the devil in seizing what God has for believers like you.

Operating in the image of God as spiritual beings moves us into His original plan.

GOD THE CREATOR

Once we understand that God is the Creator and the devil is the imitator, we don't have to fear that Christian dream interpretation or the gifts of the Spirit are vehicles to bring us into the occult (see 1 Cor. 12). God initiated our spirituality, not the devil. The occult is a mutation of what God had originally planned for us. Consider that a counterfeit Picasso painting has no value unless there is an original. Operating in the image of God as spiritual beings simply moves us into His original plan.

The Fall of humanity robbed us of this primary calling to walk and talk with God as fellow spirit-beings (see Gen. 3). However, it was not the plan of God that we should remain without a spiritual dimension. And so, through His death upon the Cross, Jesus made the way for us to fulfill our true spiritual nature. Born-again believers have been recreated to become the Spirit-led people God intended them to be (see 2 Cor. 5:17)—able to prophesy, move in the gifts of the Spirit, and interpret dreams and visions.

Is being saved enough? What else is required of us while on earth?

_____

_____

_____

_____

_____

_____

_____

_____

This is nothing new. It is what we were created to do. Jesus did not die for us that we would merely be saved, but that we would be saved, filled, and empowered by His Holy Spirit and fulfill the perfect plan that He has for us.

ALL TRUTH

Those who enter the heavenly realms using occult practices are doing so illegally, according to the Word of God, and place themselves under a curse and at enmity with God (see Lev. 20:6; Deut. 18:11-12; 1 Chron. 10:13).

Jesus told His disciples, *"...when He, the Spirit of truth, has come, He will guide you into all truth..."* (John 16:13). Jesus said that the Holy Spirit will reveal *"all truth,"* that is, the whole truth and nothing but the truth.

The devil, on the other hand, likes to feed us partial truths. You may be wondering, *What does that mean?* The devil knows that half-truths are more destructive, addictive, and convincing than blatant lies. Being deceived and anesthetized by a half-truth often keeps us away from the whole truth. How blatantly real that is!

Some people are very good at manipulating the truth. Are you guilty of this at times?

_____

_____

_____

_____

_____

_____

_____

_____

The devil has effectively swamped the spiritual arena with many half-truths, making it harder for the righteous to make it through unscathed. Every weekend we witness religious door-knockers sincerely pounding their fists trying to coerce others into their organizational web of half-truths. If you have ever tried to talk with people believing a half-truth, you have experienced the ensnarement of half-truths and the associated difficulty of breaking the mental strongholds they create.

HALF-TRUTH

Similarly, at the Fall, satan said to Eve, *"You will not surely die. For God knows that in the day you eat of it your eyes will be opened, and you will be like God..."* (Gen. 3:4-5). Now while that is partially true, it is not the whole truth. The devil, acting like the slick salesperson he is, speaks of all the benefits—and conveniently omits the consequences—of his proposal. It was true that humankind would become like God in one dimension only—choosing between good and evil. But the devil did not tell Eve and Adam that their disobedience would cause death and destruction for every future generation of humankind, tossing them into sin, suffering, and separation from Almighty God.

About twenty years ago, a female friend got saved and was born again. However, being a young Christian, she was unaware about much of the Word of God and what was right and wrong. After her conversion, the grace of God was fully on her life, yet she was robbed spiritually due to her lack of knowledge.

She had arranged to be baptized; but the week before her baptism, she went to a clairvoyant, one whom she had been consulting regularly before her salvation. The clairvoyant didn't know she was going to get baptized, but as he was giving his prophecy into her life, he told her he sensed she was going to go near water. She said, "Yes, that's true," and it drew her in. The clairvoyant said, "If you are going near water, that is dangerous. You must stay away from water." That really confused her and brought fear into her. Unfortunately, she did not get baptized but went back into the world. This is a classic example of how the enemy can reveal some truth to deceive us.

Why do people believe in and turn to those who claim to have special powers?

A similar thing happened when Jesus went into the desert after His baptism. The devil tried half-truths on the Messiah. Praise God, Jesus overcame the devil! The devil threw truth at Jesus, even using Scripture to try and deceive Him. However, as the Word of God personified (see John 1:14), Jesus, pulsing with Spirit and Life (see John 6:63), was able to outmaneuver and humiliate the enemy. Though Jesus was at the end of a forty-day fast, it was the devil who withdrew, needing respite after this encounter (see Luke 4:13).

VICTORY COMES BY LIVING THE WORD.

Jesus defeated the devil on the same grounds that you and I do—through *living* the Word, not *quoting* the Word of God. Many people can quote the Word of God, but fewer are living it! Our victory is not in knowing the Word of God, but in *Jesus, the Word of God, knowing us* (see Matt. 7:22-23). We are to absorb the Word of God to the place where it is no longer we who live, but He who lives in us (see Gal. 2:20). God is still empowering the "Word become flesh" today by His Spirit.

How keen are you at detecting someone who is deceptive and offering half-truths?

_____

_____

_____

_____

_____

_____

_____

What can you do to sharpen your gift of discernment?

_____

_____

_____

_____

_____

_____

_____

This means that in Christ, we also have overcome the world—with its lusts—and are victoriously seated, by faith, in Heaven. The Holy Spirit has also given us discernment and spiritual gifts to hear from God so that we understand all the truth (see John 16:13). When we know truth, anything short of it sets alarm bells ringing.

As believers, we have a responsibility to be immersed or baptized in the Word—through study and application—so that we can detect the faintest hint of falsity. We need not turn to the occult or New Age adherents for interpretation, because the ultimate Interpreter is "onboard" within us, and He will draw from the deposit of the Word within us to bring the correct interpretation.

SUMMARY

- Many turn to the occult for dream and vision answers, not realizing the consequences of their actions—placing themselves under a curse and at enmity with God.

- The devil is the master of imitation and deception.

- As the thief, the devil steals God's glory and the saints' inheritance.

- Going to clairvoyants or palm readers or using tarot cards, astrology, and New Age dream interpretation materials open you to counterfeit prophecy and deception.

- Jesus did not die for us merely to be saved. The infilling of the Holy Spirit allows His children to live as the true spirit beings they are destined to be.

- Dream and vision interpretation is exercising our spiritual senses in the Holy Spirit to receive our God-given inheritance.

- The devil likes to feed us half-truths. These not only deceive us, but also keep us from exploring the whole truth.

- Half-truths create mental strongholds that can spiritually rob us.

- Our victory over the devil is not in merely quoting the Word of God, but in Jesus (the Word of God) knowing us!

- When we know truth, anything short of it sets alarm bells ringing. Therefore, we have a responsibility to be immersed in the Scriptures through study and application.

PRAYER

Father, I thank You that You are releasing Your heart to me. I pray for a deeper revelation of Your Father's heart toward me. I am accepted by You. I am loved by You. I am a child of the King, an heir together with Christ. I pray that this revelation would be so great that I learn to understand the language of Heaven. I ask for a fresh anointing in wisdom. Temper me in Your wisdom, Father. May I produce the fruit of a person who is rooted and grounded in Your love. In Jesus' name, amen.

SESSION SIX REVIEW

1. The devil is _____.

    A.   the master of imitation and deception

    B.   the father of lies

    C.   a fallen angel

    D.   all of the above

2. ☐ TRUE or ☐ FALSE: The devil imitates and perverts what God has for believers.

3. Dreams are an avenue in which _____.

    A.   we can create the life we've always wanted

    B.   God can reveal His promises to us

    C.   we can claim our prosperity

    D.   None of the above

4. ☐ TRUE or ☐ FALSE: Some clairvoyants are true prophets.

5. The proper response to a dream of warning is to

    _____.

    A.   sound the alarm

    B.   embrace the fear God must be sending to you

    C.   realize the blessing of the warning and ask God how He would have you react

    D.   ignore it, as there is nothing you can do about it anyway

6. ☐ TRUE or ☐ FALSE: When we are faithful in little ways with our prophetic gift, the Lord will release greater anointing for the prophetic.

7. True born-again believers are _____.

    A.   spiritual beings

    B.   able to prophesy

    C.   empowered by the Holy Spirit

    D.   all of the above

8. The devil told half-truths to whom?

    A.   Jesus

    B.   Adam

    C.   Eve

    D.   All of the above

9. Explain how you can distinguish between the whole truth and half-truths.

Personal Application

Read through the following accounts of God speaking to people in the Bible through dreams. Decide if the main purpose of each dream was to reveal the heart, reveal promises, provide a warning, or to foretell future events.

GOD SPEAKING TO PEOPLE IN THE BIBLE THROUGH DREAMS				
	REVEAL THE HEART	REVEAL PROMISES	PROVIDE A WARNING	FORETELL THE FUTURE
Joseph Genesis 37:1-11				
Solomon 1 Kings 3:5-15				
Daniel Daniel 7:1-14				
Joseph Matthew 2:13-15				
Jacob Genesis 28:12-15				

Start a dream journal, recording your dreams upon waking each morning. Practice interpreting every dream you have.

Memorize *Colossians 3:1-2* in the Bible version of your choice.

Reading and Response

Read Chapter 7 as well as pages 194-200 of *The Divinity Code to Understanding Your Dreams and Visions* by Adam Thompson and Adrian Beale.

Summarize a few of the principles of dream interpretation that you consider to be most important.

_____

_____

_____

_____

_____

_____

DREAM NOTES

BEYOND DREAMS AND VISIONS

A blunt truth: Denying the gifts of the Holy Spirit is a blatant denial of the Word of God and a prime example of those who claim it is possible to know God apart from His Spirit.

In building a scriptural response to such a declaration, consider the following points. In twenty-one chapters, apostle John outlines the life of Jesus as God become man. Of those twenty-one chapters, which span a period of three years, almost a quarter of the book (chapters 13-17) is allocated to the upper room discourse, which took only a few hours. This stark contrast of content allocation against time says that the communion around the Last Supper is vitally important and is not captured without purpose. Prior to His departure, in the midst of that intimacy with His disciples, Jesus promised that He would send His replacement. He said, *"And I will pray the Father, and He will give you another Helper, that He may abide with you forever"* (John 14:16).

Take note how long Jesus said His replacement would be with us—*forever!* Now, considering in greater depth the words Jesus used here, we also discover that the word "another" is the Greek word *allos,* which means "another of the same quality." There is a Greek word that describes "another of different quality"—*heteros.*[1]

An illustration: If I gave you a tennis ball and then said, "I will give you another ball" and proceeded to give you a golf ball, I will have given you another (*heteros*) ball of a different kind. If I am to give you another (*allos*) of the same kind, I would have to give you another tennis ball. Therefore, in choosing to use the word *allos,* Jesus meant that He would send someone exactly the same as Himself. This means we can be absolutely sure that the Holy Spirit has come, He is of the same essence and quality as Jesus, and He is here forever. It is also not unreasonable to expect, because they are the same, that the replacement would have a ministry like the One He replaces.

> Write in your own words what you understand the previous three paragraphs to mean.

Peter's declaration that the Holy Spirit—the Promise of the Father (see Luke 24:49)—is available *"to all who are afar off"* (Acts 2:39), not only confirms Jesus' promise that this gift is not limited by time, but also confidently asserts that it is not restricted by distance either. Are we temporally or geographically distant? Then it is for us!

Our current common understanding of the word "helper" is also far from its biblical usage (see John 14:16). The word "helper" is the Greek word *parakletos*, which comes from a word which means "to speak to" and "to encourage." It describes someone who is a legal advisor or advocate.[2] This is why Jesus says in the previous verse, *"If you love Me, keep My commandments"* (John 14:15).

When we line our mouths up with revelatory truth, the Holy Spirit (as the *Parakletos*) comes forward as the representative of Christ and is empowered to operate for us while Jesus is physically absent from the world. The Spirit of Truth will only operate in the truth.

Luke uses the following sentence to open the Book of Acts: *"The former account I made, O Theophilus, of all that Jesus began both to do and teach"* (Acts 1:1). Does Luke say, "all that Jesus completed"? No! He deliberately says that his former work—the Book of Luke—only portrays what Jesus *began* to do and teach. That beginning, as seen in the ministry of Christ, is continued because the Holy Spirit is poured out so that all believers are empowered to do even greater works (see John 14:12). In using the words, *"do and teach,"* Luke also silences any ambiguity about Jesus' continued ministry through the Holy Spirit.

Gifts of the Spirit are for all people—yesterday, today, and tomorrow.

If there is proper teaching, there will also be *doing* to confirm that Word (see Mark 16:20). The Book of Acts is a confirmation and proof that Jesus has not finished, that He has not packed up shop and gone home—He is still continuing both in doing and teaching today by His Spirit. To say that the gifts of the Spirit are not for today is a statement inspired by the devil, propagated by those who seek to strengthen their own religious position (see Matt. 12:24) and who are mindful only of the things of people (see Matt. 16:23).

On a scale from one to ten, how strongly do you agree or disagree with this session's opening declaration? Explain your rating.

1	2	3	4	5	6	7	8	9	10

While most churches would not make a blatant confession like the one with which this session opens, the obvious lack of the gifts of the Spirit flowing in the Church today may indicate that we are settling for such a belief in our hearts.

GOD AWAITS

God is the Master Craftsman. He is capable of engineering the events in people's lives with incredible precision. The Bible is full of examples of what may look like just a random sequence of occurrences that then turn out to prefigured events in the life of Christ. Some examples are the life of Joseph (discussed briefly earlier), Abraham's offering up of Isaac on Mount Moriah (see Genesis 22:1-19), and the death and resurrection of Jonah, to name a few. One such sequence in the life of Christ reveals truth about the Holy Spirit that we will discuss now.

John's Gospel records that after Jesus had fed the five thousand, He perceived that the people would come and take Him by force and make Him king (see John 6:15). This same Scripture says that when Jesus saw what was about to happen, He departed alone to the mountain. This action is very significant.

> **Why did Jesus choose to go alone to the mountain?**

_____

_____

_____

_____

_____

_____

_____

_____

_____

_____

There was to be a day when Jesus would accept the people's accolades as their King, but this was not it. That day was yet to come and was manifest as the day of His triumphant entry into Jerusalem (see Luke 19:37-40). The prophet Daniel records that day in prophecy with pinpoint accuracy. He says that recognition of Meshiach Nagid (Messiah King) would take place 173,880 days[3] from the date of the decree to rebuild Jerusalem (see Dan. 9:25-26). On the exact day prophesied by Daniel, Jesus entered Jerusalem, accepted recognition as their King, and was subsequently executed as the nation's substitutionary sacrifice. This is all recorded in Daniel's prophecy.

Therefore, when John records that Jesus went up the mountain alone, he is showing us something deeper. In Mark's account of this episode, he tells us that Jesus made His disciples get into the boat and go before Him to the other side, and then He went up the mountain to pray (see Mark 6:45-46). John adds, *"Now when evening came, His disciples went down to the sea"* (John 6:16).

If we make a parallel between going up the mount and Jesus entering Heaven (see Heb. 8:5), recognize that evening is a metaphor for Jesus' departure (see John 9:4-5), and also note that Jesus is praying for His disciples in Heaven (see Heb. 7:25-26; Rom. 8:34), an incredible insight is revealed to us.

In outline, we see:

* Jesus broken as the Bread of Life (see John 6:35)

* Jesus feeding an inordinate number of people

* Jesus being proclaimed King

* Jesus rising up into Heaven

* Jesus' physical absence from the earth

* Jesus praying for His disciples

* The disciples making their way across the sea of humanity

Do you see that the above events are a prophetic prefiguring of what was about to happen?

103

Therefore, when Jesus comes down to His disciples and observes their struggle rowing (see Mark 6:48), we see His current response to our own need when we are likewise working in our own strength.

As eye-opening as that may be, what is even more remarkable is what Mark next records: "... *Now about the fourth watch of the night He came to them, walking on the sea, and would have passed them by*" (Mark 6:48). Jesus sees their struggle *"and would have passed them by."* What was He doing? Couldn't He see their need? What was He waiting for?

Let's consider also how He appeared to them on the sea. Mark says, *"But when they saw Him walking upon the sea, they supposed it had been a spirit, and cried out"* (Mark 6:49 KJV). They perceived Jesus as a spirit, a point echoed in Matthew's Gospel, but they were mistaken because Jesus was physically walking on the water. It is no coincidence that their misconception is recorded because this is how Jesus passes by us today, as the Holy Spirit.

Stop and think about that for a moment. What is He waiting for? He is waiting for a faith-filled invitation (see Matt. 14:28) and a ceasing from our own works of the flesh (see John 6:21) before He enters our boat.

Is God waiting for your invitation so He can enter your boat, that is, your life?

_____

_____

_____

_____

_____

_____

_____

_____

Are you ready to stop struggling in your own strength and enlist His help in every situation and challenge?

_____

_____

_____

_____

_____

_____

_____

_____

Jesus reinforces this truth when He appears, unexpected and unrecognized, after His death, to two disciples on their way to Emmaus (see Luke 24:13-31). The Bible records:

> _Then they drew near to the village whee they were going, and He indicated that He would have gone farther. But they constrained Him, saying, "Abide with us, for it is toward evening, and the day is far spent." And He went in to stay with them_ (Luke 24:28-29).

How amazing! After achieving the greatest victory in the history of humankind—resurrection from the dead—Jesus is awaiting an invitation before entering into communion with His disciples. Only in the light of the forthcoming ministry of the Holy Spirit can we fully explain this anomaly. It illustrates the disciples' ignorance and emphasizes their need for sensitivity. The truth here is that although the Holy Spirit is incredibly powerful, we are in need of heightened spiritual awareness to commune with Him.

AN AWAKENING

This is a lesson that is seen in the life of Elijah. Elijah had a tremendous victory on Mount Carmel, a victory that included calling down fire, killing 450 false prophets, breaking a three-year drought through prayer, and outrunning the king's chariot (see 1 Kings 18:19-46). Yet, in the very next chapter, we see God contrasting power with the inner voice of the Holy Spirit to break a wrong mind-set within Elijah. The Scripture records:

> _Then He said, "Go out, and stand on the mountain before the Lord." And behold, the Lord passed by, and a great and strong wind tore into the mountains and broke the rocks in pieces before the Lord, but the Lord was not in the wind; and after the wind an earthquake, but the Lord was not in the earthquake; and after the earthquake a fire, but the Lord was not in the fire; and after the fire a still small voice_ (1 Kings 19:11-12).

Like Elijah, we can be so caught up with the ministry or the manifestation of God's power that we miss the need for relationship with Him. As in all relationships, it is only in heart-to-heart communication that we truly hear what the other is saying.

Only in heart-to-heart communication do we truly hear what the other is saying.

Sensitivity to the Holy Spirit is developed when there is less room in our own hearts for self. Elijah had a fixation that he was the last godly man standing (see 1 Kings 19:10,14). This was a wrong mind-set, brought to the surface by Jezebel's death threat, which took advantage of his burnout due to being overworked in the ministry. God's mighty demonstration of power to Elijah highlights the need to appreciate the distinction between a manifestation of God and God Himself.

In light of this, we are always to remember that visions and dreams—as a manifestation of the power of God—are not an end in themselves and, though they lead us in the purposes of God, they are ultimately to direct us deeper in our relationship with the Holy Spirit.

Following this object lesson, God commissions Elijah to anoint two kings and Elisha. It is interesting to see that Elijah caught what God was trying to convey because, like Enoch before him, he was taken up as one who walked with God (see Gen. 5:24). Perhaps more revealing is the fact that Elijah did not personally anoint the two kings, Hazael and Jehu, as he was commissioned by God to do, but that Elisha, his understudy, did (see 2 Kings 8:13-15; 9:1-3).

What does that say? It says that in getting closer to God, Elijah poured his life into his successor. In doing that, he created and developed an unquenchable hunger and sensitivity for the Holy Spirit in Elisha. This hunger was openly displayed on the day in which Elijah was taken up. (If you haven't read Second Kings 2:1-14 recently, please stop here and take the time to familiarize yourself with its contents.[4])

This was an appetite that would not stop for repeated offers of rest or be dissuaded by the voice of his peers (see 2 Kings 2:2-6). He would not settle for conversion (symbolized by *Gilgal*) nor be content at coming into the House of God (symbolized by *Bethel*). Under Elijah's training, Elisha developed such hunger that he would not be satisfied merely with a demonstration of God's power (symbolized by their trip to *Jericho*). He was prepared to lay down his life (*Jordan*, which means "descender" or "death") and was rewarded with a double portion of the Holy Spirit!

THE COST

Somehow, we read about the great exploits of Old and New Testament saints and even of Christ Himself, and yet we forget the cost. Considering Jesus for a moment, while we recognize and reverence Him as the God-Man, it is important to remember that He did not perform His miracles as God, but as a man. The miracles He worked were those of a man empowered by the Holy Spirit, to show us how it is done. Yes, that's right. He was as totally reliant upon the Holy Spirit for ministry as we are. Why else did He need to be anointed? As Luke records:

The Spirit of the Lord is upon Me, because He has anointed Me to preach the gospel to the poor; He has sent Me to heal the brokenhearted, to proclaim liberty to the captives and recovery of sight to the blind, to set at liberty those who are oppressed; to proclaim the acceptable year of the Lord (Luke 4:18-19).

And elsewhere it says:

How God anointed Jesus of Nazareth with the Holy Spirit and with power, who went about doing good and healing all who were oppressed by the devil, for God was with Him (Acts 10:38).

It is easy to lose sight of the fact that as a man (like all the Old Testament greats before Him), Jesus needed an anointing of the Holy Spirit to minister—an anointing birthed and renewed in prayer. Again, in Luke, the Gospel that speaks about Jesus as a man, we read:

When all the people were baptized, it came to pass that Jesus also was baptized; and while He prayed, the heaven was opened. And the Holy Spirit descended... (Luke 3:21-22).

The anointing is poured out in prayerful relationship. It is no coincidence that we see Jesus in prayer—in the wilderness (see Luke 5:16), before He chose His disciples (see Luke 6:12), before Peter's confession of faith (see Luke 9:18), at the transfiguration (see Luke 9:28-29), before teaching His disciples to pray (see Luke 11:1), and after feeding the five thousand (see Matt. 14:23)—and it should be noted that on the night of Jesus' betrayal that Judas knew where to find Him because He often withdrew to that place to pray (see Luke 22:39; John 18:2). It was not so much that He went to prayer because He was about to minister, but rather that His ministry flowed out of His relationship with God, as marked by prayer.

Do you sometimes lose sight of the fact that Jesus needed God's anointing of the Holy Spirit to carry out His destiny?

_____

_____

_____

_____

_____

_____

_____

Do you sometimes lose sight of the fact that *you* need God's anointing of the Holy Spirit to fulfill *your* destiny?

_____

_____

_____

_____

_____

_____

_____

Not only does the Bible record that Jesus prayed, but it also captures His *desire* for prayer: "*Now in the morning, having risen a long while before daylight, He went out and departed to a solitary place; and there He prayed*" (Mark 1:35). And on another occasion, He "*continued all night in prayer to God*" (Luke 6:12). Jesus was passionate about prayer. It was like oxygen to Him.

Sadly, we lack that fervency today. Many mistakenly believe that it was different for Jesus and that we could never attain His level of ministry. That is a lie that hampers our spiritual progress. For the most part, we are like the disciples in the Garden of Gethsemane: our spirits are willing, but the flesh is weak.

How true is it in your life—that your spirit is willing to pray, but when the time comes, other "things" march into your schedule and invade your mind?

Through Scripture and personal experience, it is confirmed that the presence of the Holy Spirit is with us today. We have discussed the need for increased sensitivity to commune with Him, and we have seen the difference between a manifestation of God and God Himself. We have also explored how this revelation comes with a call to a deeper personal relationship with God. We recognize the cost of a prayerful relationship with our heavenly Father for the anointing we seek.

IN THE MIRROR

It has been long said that the New Testament is in the Old Testament *concealed*, and the Old Testament is in the New Testament *revealed*. The premise on which this statement is based is that the New Testament opens Old Testament truth that was previously hidden from human understanding. While this is true, it is also worth noting that the Old Testament in its physical and positional "types" opens to us deeper understanding of our spiritual standing in the New Testament.

To take this discussion further, it is worth looking at several very revealing parallels in the Old Testament to appreciate where we stand in the plan and purposes of God today.

Moses, Joshua, and Judges

Moses led the people of Israel out of Egypt, but it was Joshua who led them into the Promised Land. Although Joshua began to clear Canaan of opposition forces, the Bible also records that:

> *Yet the children of Manasseh could not drive out the inhabitants of those cities, but the Canaanites were determined to dwell in that land. And it happened, when the children of Israel grew strong, that they put the Canaanites to forced labor, but did not utterly drive them out* (Joshua 17:12-13).

The Book of Judges follows Joshua and describes this same inability to push home the advantage gained through Joshua's invasion:

> *But the children of Benjamin did not drive out the Jebusites who inhabited Jerusalem; so the Jebusites dwell with the children of Benjamin in Jerusalem to this day* (Judges 1:21).

The first chapter of the Book of Judges records this failure to drive out the inhabitants by the respective tribes: Ephraim, Zebulun, Asher, Naphtali, and Dan (see Judg. 1:29-34). Why did they fail to take hold of all that God had promised them? In the next chapter, we read:

> *And you shall make no covenant with the inhabitants of this land; you shall tear down their altars. But you have not obeyed My voice. Why have you done this? Therefore I also said, "I will not drive them out before you; but they shall be thorns in your side, and their gods shall be a snare to you"* (Judges 2:2-3).

The reason that *Israel failed* in their conquest was that *they began to settle down and relax when the job was only half done.* They embraced the values of the society around them and paid dearly for their spiritual apathy.

Is there a job that God gave you to do and you stopped when only half finished? What will it take for you to complete your task for Him?

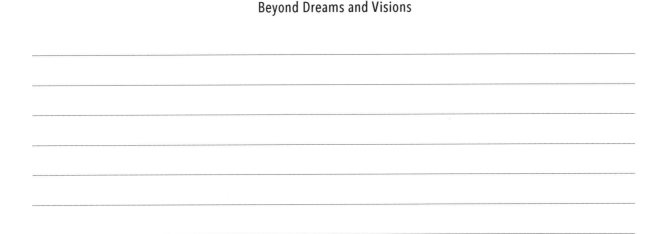

Elijah, Elisha, and Gehazi

As already discussed, Elijah passed on the mantle to Elisha, who received a double portion of the Spirit that was upon his mentor. Likewise, Elisha was preparing someone to whom he would pass the baton—Gehazi. However, after God had healed Naaman the leper through the ministry of Elisha, Gehazi went after Naaman to receive the reward his master had turned down (see 2 Kings 5:20-27). On Gehazi's return to Elisha, his master's words to him are particularly enlightening. Elisha says to Gehazi:

> ...Did not my heart go with you when the man turned back from his chariot to meet you? Is it time to receive money and to receive clothing, olive groves and vineyards, sheep and oxen, male and female servants? (2 Kings 5:26).

As indicated by the words, *"Is it time,"* Gehazi had no idea where he stood in the purposes of God. He also had no appreciation of the anointing he would have received if only he had not sought material security.

John the Baptist, Jesus, and...?

Now to bring this closer to home, Jesus said that the ministry of John the Baptist was a parallel to that of Elijah. Speaking of John, Jesus said, *"And if you are willing to receive it, he is Elijah who is to come"* (Matt. 11:14). And He also said:

> But I say to you that Elijah has come already, and they did not know him.... Then the disciples understood that He spoke to them of John the Baptist (Matthew 17:12-13).

John held a parallel spiritual role to that of Elijah. It was not by chance that Jesus' baptism took place in the Jordan, the same place where Elijah passed on the mantle to Elisha. And the Jordan was also the place through which Joshua would lead the children of Israel so they could enter their Promised Land. Like Moses before him, John prepared the people by leading them in renewal in the wilderness so they could come into the Kingdom being opened by Christ (see Matt. 4:17, 12:28).

It is no coincidence that the name Joshua is the Old Testament equivalent of the name Jesus in the New Testament. Moses and Elijah are a type of John the Baptist. Joshua and Elisha were prefigures of Jesus. Gehazi holds the same position as the children of Israel in the Book of Judges, but who holds this position today? To whom did Jesus pass the mantle on? Answer: the Church—the universal Church of believers worldwide!

> Was God forewarning us that the Church, like the children of Israel, is prone to embracing the world and stopping short of God's will?

ENTRY VERSUS CONQUEST

Are you asking, "But didn't Jesus do it all for us?" To answer that question, let's go back to Joshua's crossing of the Jordan River. The Scriptures record that Joshua said, *"Behold, the ark of the covenant of the Lord of all the earth is crossing over before you into the Jordan"* (Josh. 3:11).

What did the ark have in it? It had the two tablets of stone containing the Ten Commandments, Aaron's rod that budded, and a piece of the manna from the wilderness. The tablets represent the Word of God, Aaron's rod represents resurrection, and the manna represents the bread of the wilderness. Who is the Word of God, the Resurrection, and the Bread of Life? Jesus is all three! So, the ark here represents Jesus.

What does *Jordan* mean? Jordan means "descender" or "death." So, the ark entering into the Jordan represents Jesus passing into death. What happened when the feet of the priests who were carrying the ark touched the waters of the Jordan?

...the waters which came down from upstream stood still, and rose in a heap very far away [all the way back to] at Adam, the city that is beside Zaretan. So the waters that went down into the Sea of the Arabah, the Salt Sea, failed, and were cut off; and the people crossed over opposite Jericho (Joshua 3:16).

When the anointed bearers of the ark entered the river, the water retreated all the way back to a town called Adam. If we recognize that *"the wages of sin is death..."* (Rom. 6:23) and that it is no coincidence that the town was called Adam, we will realize that we are foreseeing physically a spiritual truth yet to happen in Christ's death upon the cross. When Jesus entered into death (the Jordan), the flow of sin was rolled back to Adam. Hallelujah!

Is this a new realization for you? Do you need to take a moment or two to absorb the correlation between the two events? Write what you are thinking about.

The children of Israel subsequently built a memorial with twelve stones, which represent the twelve apostles (see Matt. 16:18), and then symbolically cut off the flesh through circumcision before proceeding into the Promised Land.

Was the Promised Land given to them through the ark, causing them to cross over on dry ground? Yes and no. Yes, God had made a way, and no, they had to clear the land as they were led by God (see Josh. 5:14-15).

As told in the Book of Judges, Israel failed to press home their advantage. Flanked by fear, they chose rather to embrace the society they were sent to conquer. Today, we can see whether Jesus has done it all for us by looking at the equivalent of land clearing and simply asking ourselves a rhetorical question: *Are people still oppressed of the devil, and are people still unsaved in our world?*

God has cleared the way—receive all that He has for us!

Jesus would have passed the disciples by, and likewise the Holy Spirit is walking past our boat right now. But could it be that, like Gehazi, we are prone to miss where we stand on God's timeline and find ourselves clamoring for superficial security in our homes, cars, and retirement plans?

Like Elisha before us, we cannot afford to be content just to arrive at conversion (Gilgal), to stop at the house of God (Bethel), or to be satisfied by a display of God's power (Jericho). Rather, let us cut off the flesh (crossing over the Jordan) and push in to receive all the Spirit that Jesus has for us! Don't forget that Jesus has said:

> *Very truly I tell you, whoever believes in Me will do the works I have been doing, and they will do even greater things than these, because I am going to the Father* (John 14:12 NIV).

In these words, Jesus is promising us a double portion of His Spirit.

Are you as hungry for the Spirit of your Master as Elisha was?

Are you prepared like Elisha for the tests of perseverance?

Or are you comfortable just to adopt the fatalistic stance of your peers?

We can and should get excited about dreams and visions, but we are not to settle here. God has so much more for us than we could ever imagine. Dreams and visions are only catalysts to awaken and revitalize a sensitivity and hunger within us for the Holy Spirit.

Lifting our spiritual eyes, we see that there is a Kingdom to be won and the offer of a double portion of anointing to lead us into complete victory.

Have the truths in this guide created within you a passion for the Holy Spirit that will not be satisfied with anything less than the fullness of God?

Summary

* The Holy Spirit is exactly like Jesus and comes to complete the work that Jesus began.

* The Promise of the Father (the Holy Spirit) is available to everyone, independent of distance and time.

* Wherever there is correct teaching, there will be people doing the works of Christ.

* The ministry of Christ outlines the ministry of the Holy Spirit today.

* One series of events sets out:
  * Jesus broken as the Bread of Life
  * Jesus feeding an inordinately large number of people
  * Jesus being proclaimed King
  * Jesus going into Heaven
  * Jesus' physical absence from the earth
  * Jesus praying for His disciples
  * The disciples struggling in their own strength across the sea of humanity
  * Jesus coming to them as the Holy Spirit
  * The need for increased sensitivity in dealing with the Holy Spirit

* Although the Holy Spirit is incredibly powerful, we are in need of increased sensitivity to commune with Him.

* The life of Elijah illustrates the importance of distinguishing between a manifestation of God and God Himself.

* Dreams and visions are manifestations of God; they are not ends in themselves. They are to direct us into a deeper relationship with God.

* The miracles Jesus performed were as a man anointed by the Holy Spirit, to show us how it is done.

* The anointing is poured out in prayerful relationship.

* Moses led the children of Israel out of Egypt. Joshua led them into the Promised Land. The Book of Judges shows us that Israel failed to take all the land; they embraced the world they were supposed to conquer.

- Elijah passed on the anointing to Elisha. However, Elisha's servant and would-be replacement—Gehazi—failed to understand his time by clamoring after material security.

- John the Baptist led the people in preparation for Jesus' ministry. Jesus led the people into the Promised Land and in turn passed the baton on to the Church. The Church, like its predecessors—Judges and Gehazi—has stopped short of what God intended for her!

- There remains a job to be done; people are still going to hell! We cannot camp on Jesus' accomplishments. The Holy Spirit wants to lead us into more so that we can complete the work. We are not to get hung up on dreams and visions; they are only a means to help us complete the conquest of bringing the Promised Land to others.

PRAYER

I surrender my mind to You, Father. I repent of any unholy meditation and ask for a sanctified imagination. I pray for the Holy Spirit to illuminate any place in my heart where I may be seeking after signs rather than intimacy with You. I desire to see Your name glorified in the earth, and to this end I ask that You would use me. In Jesus' name, amen!

NOTES

1. *"Heteros,"* *Blue Letter Bible*, accessed August 30, 2011, https://www.blueletterbible.org/lang/lexicon/lexicon.cfm?t=kjv&strongs=g2087.

2. "Helper," *Merriam-Webster Dictionary*, accessed August 30, 2011, http://www.merriam-webster.com/dictionary/helper.

3. In working through Daniel's prophecy (see Dan. 9:25-26), we need to consider that:

   * All the ancient calendars were based on a 360-day year.

   * Sixty-nine weeks speaks of sixty-nine weeks of years. The Hebrews had a week of days, a week of weeks, a week of months, and a week of years (see Lev. 25:1-22; 26:33-35).

   * Therefore, sixty-nine weeks = 69 x 7 x 360 = 173,880 days.

   * For a complete breakdown of Daniel's prophecy, see Chuck Missler, *Cosmic Codes: Hidden Messages from the Edge of Eternity* (Idaho: Koinonia House, 2004), 235f.

4. Gilgal means "circle of stones" and was the first camp of Israel after crossing the Jordan River (see Josh. 4:19-20). It is the place where Joshua renewed the rite of covenant by circumcising all the males born in the wilderness and thus *"rolled away the reproach of Egypt"* (see Josh. 5:2-9; Josh. 5:9). Gilgal, therefore, symbolizes the rolling away of the heart of stone and the beginning of the life of faith. Bethel means "House of God" and symbolizes the new home in which we have been adopted as heirs. Jericho is the place of Israel's first victory in Canaan and is also known as the City of Palms (see Deut. 34:3). It therefore symbolizes the victory we come into by exercising the Word of God (see Rev. 12:11). Jordan means "descender" or "death." The journey Gilgal ➔ Bethel ➔ Jericho ➔ Jordan therefore depicts the walk of faith from the new birth to glory. The fact that Elisha receives a double portion of anointing suggests that this is also a depiction of his path to maturity in the Spirit!

SESSION SEVEN REVIEW

1. According to John 14:16, what did Jesus promise His disciples?

    A. A boatload of fish

    B. Healing

    C. Another Helper

    D. An easy life

2. What can we be sure of regarding the Holy Spirit?

    A. He has the same essence as Jesus

    B. He is with us forever

    C. He has the same quality as Jesus

    D. All of the above

3. What is the opposite of faith?

    A. Doubt

    B. Fear

    C. Unbelief

    D. Confusion

4. ☐ TRUE or ☐ FALSE: The Holy Spirit is also our Encourager, our *Parakletos*.

5. ☐ TRUE or ☐ FALSE: Some believers are empowered to do even greater works than Jesus did.

6. Why did Jesus go up into the mountain by Himself after feeding more than five thousand people?

    A. He wanted to avoid premature kingship

    B. He was tired

    C. He was afraid of the crowd

    D. He needed to pray

7. ☐ TRUE or ☐ FALSE: Jesus waits for us to invite Him into our lives.

8. Sensitivity to the Holy Spirit is developed
    when _____.
    A. we rid our hearts of self
    B. we commit to periods of fasting
    C. we are physically and mentally exhausted

9. ☐ TRUE or ☐ FALSE: Dreams and visions are not manifestations of God.

10. What is the mature believer's perspective on dreams and visions?

_____

_____

_____

_____

_____

_____

_____

_____

_____

_____

Personal Application

Read *Hebrews 12*.

Ask the Holy Spirit to reveal any ungodly imaginations that you might be engaging. Be quick to respond to the Holy Spirit and shut down any thoughts about which you feel convicted.

Continue to practice dream interpretation. As you continue to keep your dream journal, practice this week on a friend. Talk to a close friend or your spouse—someone who loves you and is gracious with and encouraging to you—about your desire to be used by the Lord in dream interpretation. Ask if he or she will help you practice by telling you about a dream he or she has had recently. Remember the things you have learned. Begin by asking the Lord for wisdom. Ask for context (refer to previous sessions if you need to refresh your memory). Only after considering and praying, consult outside sources such as *The Divinity Code*.

Memorize *Psalm 24:7-8*.

Reading and Response

Read Chapter 8 as well as pages 201-207 of *The Divinity Code to Understanding Your Dreams and Visions* by Adam Thompson and Adrian Beale.

What are the main differences between Elisha (Elijah's protégé) and Gehazi (Elisha's protégé)?

_____

_____

_____

_____

_____

_____

_____

_____

_____

_____

_____

_____

_____

_____

_____

_____

_____

DREAM NOTES

THE LANGUAGE OF DREAMS

It is important to point out that there is no formula for interpreting dreams. It is more about cultivating a relationship with the Holy Spirit than applying a series of rules for interpreting. This is because God the Holy Spirit is the Author of dreams:

> *...God has shown Pharaoh [through his dreams] what He is about to do* (Genesis 41:28).

> *And the dream...is established by God, and God will shortly bring it to pass* (Genesis 41:32).

> *For God does speak—now one way, now another—though no one perceives it. In a dream, in a vision of the night, when deep sleep falls on people as they slumber in their beds* (Job 33:14-15 NIV).

> *Then, being divinely warned in a dream...* (Matthew 2:12).

> *...And being warned by God in a dream...* (Matthew 2:22).

God the Holy Spirit is also the Interpreter of dreams:

> *But there is a God in heaven who reveals secrets, and He has made known...your dream, and the visions of your head upon your bed...* (Daniel 2:28).

> *...Do not interpretations belong to God?...* (Genesis 40:8).

...because I know that the Spirit of the Holy God is in you, and no secret troubles you, explain to me the visions of my dream that I have seen, and its interpretation (Daniel 4:9).

However, having established this truth and the additional important truth that anyone who wants to interpret dreams needs to have a foundation in the Scriptures, there are some individual principles that are important to understand and that will assist you in opening God's messages through dreams:

* Metaphorical or literal

* Context

* Meditate on a dream

* Sequence

* Past, present, and future

* Recurring dreams

* Feelings

* Gender

* Names

* Numbers

* Local, national, and cultural idiosyncrasies

* Practical advice

Before delving into these principles, it is important to understand a Kingdom truth that strengthens us in the Word and the Spirit: *spiritual understanding* is not a mental faculty; it *is a dimension of the heart*. This is highlighted when Jesus explains the Parable of the Sower. He says:

When anyone hears the word of the kingdom, and does not understand it, then the wicked one comes and snatches away what was sown in his heart. This is he who received seed by the wayside (Matthew 13:19).

Here Jesus links the heart with understanding, explaining that a heart that lacks understanding is vulnerable to becoming unproductive. Jesus further explains two other soil types—stony and thorn ridden—and then He says:

But the seed falling on good soil refers to someone who hears the word and understands it. This is the one who produces a crop, yielding a hundred, sixty or thirty times what was sown (Matthew 13:23 NIV).

Notice that both the unproductive and productive soil types *hear* the Word. The difference is *understanding*. This verse says that we will only bear fruit when we are applying the Word of God to our lives. And since the gift of the Holy Spirit is conditional on obedience (see John 14:15-16), we are not going to be able to interpret fruitfully without applying the Word to our hearts.

METAPHORICAL OR LITERAL

It is imperative to recognize that the vast majority of dreams are metaphors. They come as parables, riddles, and puzzles to be decoded. Of the more than twenty dreams recorded in Scripture, twelve of them are symbolic in nature. That is, sixty percent are metaphors, and the remaining forty percent are literal (see table 2). Literal dreams do not require interpretation because they do not consist of symbolic images. In our experience, the percentage of parable-type dreams is higher today than in Bible times. This is probably because the Holy Spirit has been poured out and the Bible is more readily available.

The majority of dreams come as parables.

As the majority of dreams come as parables, a very common mistake is to disregard such dreams because they utilize elements of something to which we have recently been exposed. Say, for example, I find a bee floating in the dishwater in the kitchen sink, and that night I dream about a swarm of bees. If I wake and say to myself, *I had that dream because of that bee in the sink last night,* and then dismiss it as nonsense, I have missed God's voice. This is because God takes the opportunity to use the images to which we have been freshly exposed to give us new perspectives on our spiritual walk.

Just as Jesus related to fishermen with net casting (see Matt. 4:19), to farmers with seed sowing (see Matt. 13:1-9), and to a strongly relational society with scenes of marriage (see Matt. 22:37-39), so the Holy Spirit loves to use images fresh in our memories, often throwing in abstract elements and people we know to convey truth.

Is the Western Church being lulled into a false security? (See Revelation 3:17-18.)

_____

_____

_____

_____

Have we gradually become spectators of the Gospel instead of bearers of its life-giving message?

_____

_____

_____

_____

_____

Are we worshiping God or the riffs and melodies of the music we have created to do so?

_____

_____

_____

_____

_____

_____

If these questions and issues raise concerns, then it is evident that we need a new level of sensitivity to the Spirit of God and His Word, especially as they come to us in dreams.

God is waiting for the Church to reawaken spiritual sensitivity so that He can give the world dreams for Him to interpret through us, dreams that will confirm His reality. There is, therefore, a need for a "School of the Prophets" in which to grow and develop that spiritual sensitivity. Sadly, without a prophetic edge, we continually revert to the systems of people to build the Church.

Does the bee dream sound weird? Perhaps, but no weirder than a dream in which seven emaciated cows come up out of a river and eat seven fat cows (see Gen. 41:20), or a dream in which a man's heart is ripped out and replaced by an animal's heart (see Dan. 4:16).

Learn to ask the Spirit of God what He is telling you. Does He say, "Too much pizza!" or "There's truth in these dreams"? Don't disregard any dream, no matter how bizarre. God can speak to you through it.

How quick are you to dismiss a dream?

As the majority of our dreams are metaphors, they are more likely to convey a spiritual parallel. A wildfire is more likely to indicate judgment or anger, and a car accident is probably a warning of a potential family, ministry, or business mishap or conflict.

The table below contains a list of most of the dreams recorded in the Bible, who is involved, the Bible reference, whether the dream is metaphoric or literal, the nature of the dream, and pertinent comments. You will find the information interesting and helpful when understanding dreams from God.

GUIDE TO DREAMS

	DREAMS RECORDED IN THE BIBLE				
NUMBER	PERSON	REFERENCE	M/L*	NATURE	COMMENTS
1	Abimelech	Gen. 20:3-7	L	Warning	Protecting Sarah, threat of death
2	Jacob	Gen. 28:12-15	M	Promise	Ladder (see John 1:51), land, descendants, Presence of God, fulfill Word
3	Jacob	Gen. 31:10-13	L	Directive	Confirmed current situation, then gave direction to go to Canaan
4	Laban	Gen. 31:24	L	Warning	God protecting Jacob
5	Joseph	Gen. 37:5-7	M	Promise	Leadership over brothers
6	Joseph	Gen. 37:9	M	Promise	Leadership over family
7	Butler	Gen. 40:9-11	M	Promise	Resurrection promise (faith)
8	Baker	Gen. 40:16-17	M	Judgment	Judgment promise (works)
9	Pharaoh	Gen. 41:1-7	M	Warning	Two angles of the same situation (see Gen. 41:25)
10	Midianite	Judg. 7:13-14	M	Warning	Weakened recipients, strengthened faith in Gideon
11	Solomon	1 Kings 3:5-15	L	Promise	Requested a hearing heart
12	Nebuchadnezzar	Dan. 2:31-35	M	Future events	Forgot dream (see Dan. 2:5)
13	Nebuchadnezzar	Dan. 4:10-18	M	Warning	Judgment for pride—seven years; God rules and gives to whomever He wills
14	Daniel	Dan. 7:1-14	M	Future events	Wrote the dream (see Dan. 7:1)
15	Joseph	Matt. 1:20-23	L	Directive	To marry Mary
16	Wise Men	Matt. 2:12	M	Directive	Warning about Herod's jealousy and to return home another way
17	Joseph	Matt. 2:13	L	Directive	Angel warns about Herod's attempt to kill Jesus and directs him to flee to Egypt
18	Joseph	Matt. 2:19-20	L	Directive	Angel directs him to Israel

DREAMS RECORDED IN THE BIBLE					
NUMBER	PERSON	REFERENCE	M/L*	NATURE	COMMENTS
19	Joseph	Matt. 2:22	L	Directive	Warning to go into Galilee
20	Pilate's wife	Matt. 27:19	M	Warning	Warned of suffering because of their part in the judgment of Jesus

CONTEXT

Just as it is important to consider whether you are looking at a metaphoric or a literal dream, it is equally important to consider the context of the dream. Dreams need to be interpreted with consideration for the environment in which they occur. Accurately interpreting a dream with only one element is not possible. Without the entire dream and some understanding of the circumstances surrounding the dreamer, an accurate picture is unlikely.

Let's consider a biblical example. Suppose we are pondering the meaning of a particular character in a Scripture passage—let's say Jacob. When Jacob is on his way back into Canaan, just before he meets his brother Esau, he has an encounter with God at Peniel (see Gen. 32:22-32). God wrestles with Jacob to get a confession from, and a revelation to, him. A pivotal point comes in this encounter and is recorded in the following way: *"So He said to him, 'What is your name?' He said, 'Jacob.' And He said, 'Your name shall no longer be called Jacob, but Israel...'"* (Gen. 32:27-28).

Jacob has to come to understand who he is. His name literally means "Grabber, swindler, or supplanter"; it describes someone who is out for only himself. This picture is confirmed in Scripture as Jacob steals both the birthright and the blessing from his brother Esau. It continues as we see him working as hard as he can to cheat a bigger swindler, Laban, when Laban's flocks are conceiving (see Gen. 30:37-42).

God asked his name? Surely He already knew! But He asked him his name so that Jacob would make a confession and receive a revelation. This is the same confession you and I need to make to come to God. We first need to see ourselves as sinners. Sin has its root in selfishness, so sins are the things we do without consideration of others (see Isa. 53:6).

If sin has its root in selfishness, what is the root of selflessness?

....

....

....

_____

_____

_____

_____

_____

What characteristic best describes how you act on a daily basis?

_____

_____

_____

_____

_____

_____

In saying his name, Jacob says, "I'm for myself only!" After that confession, God, through His grace, says, "You shall no longer be called 'Swindler,' but 'Israel,'" which means "a prince with God." Jacob is a picture of the fleshly person—the old self—who is only out for himself despite any self-righteous acts he may perform. When God said, "He will be called 'Israel,'" God was calling him to live according to the spiritual person. From this point on, whenever we see Jacob and Israel mentioned, Jacob represents the fleshly person in action, and Israel the spiritual person.

Just as the meaning of Jacob is dependent on whom he is mentioned with in Scripture, so the meaning of an element of a dream is dependent on its surroundings. The principle of considering the context, therefore, teaches us that the elements of interpretation of one dream are not necessarily transferable to another. The context of the dream will influence the meaning. What is going on in the life of the dreamer also needs to be considered as context.

MEDITATE ON A DREAM

It is always best to take your time and meditate on a dream in its entirety before coming to a conclusion about its interpretation, particularly with longer ones. Daniel applied this principle when interpreting Nebuchadnezzar's dreams:

"This dream I, King Nebuchadnezzar, have seen. Now you, Belteshazzar, declare its interpretation, since all the wise men of my kingdom are not able to make known to me the interpretation; but you are able, for the Spirit of the Holy God is in you." Then Daniel, whose name was Belteshazzar, was astonished for a time, and his thoughts troubled him... (Daniel 4:18-19).

There are at least *three good reasons* for taking our time with an interpretation. First, we need to see the overall image God is conveying in the dream. We may have individual elements pegged for certain parts of the dream, but until we can see the larger picture, we will not know how they fit what God has mapped out. It is easy to be led into false interpretation as we move from the elements to the whole. We must also consider how the whole affects the elements if we are to get a true interpretation.

Second, we must take our time to "see" the dream. What I am trying to relate is that we need to look through, or past, the scenes and actions of the dream to gain understanding. For example, Jeremiah was directed to view the potter before God had him deliver His message to Israel:

The word which came to Jeremiah from the Lord, saying: "Arise and go down to the potter's house, and there I will cause you to hear My words." Then I went down to the potter's house, and there he was, making something at the wheel. And the vessel that he made of clay was marred in the hand of the potter; so he made it again into another vessel, as it seemed good to the potter to make. Then the word of the Lord came to me, saying, "O house of Israel, can I not do with you as this potter?" says the Lord. "Look, as the clay is in the potter's hand, so are you in My hand, O house of Israel" (Jeremiah 18:1-6).

Just as Jeremiah gained a heightened understanding of God's desired message to Israel by observing the potter, so we need to look beyond the mere words of the dream to "see" what message God is conveying through all the scenes.

The third reason to take our time is so that we can seek God's wisdom in knowing how to deliver the interpretation to the dreamer. It is one thing to have an interpretation; it is another to know what action the dreamer should take after discerning it.

Are you planning to use your newfound gift of dream interpretation on your own dreams only?

_____

_____

_____

_____

_____

Are you going to offer your gift to others?

_____

_____

_____

_____

_____

_____

_____

Joseph, when giving the interpretation of Pharaoh's dreams, is a classic example of having the wisdom to bring the solution to the problem. Filled with the Spirit of God, he said:

> *Now therefore, let Pharaoh select a discerning and wise man, and set him over the land of Egypt. Let Pharaoh do this, and let him appoint officers over the land, to collect one-fifth of the produce of the land of Egypt in the seven plentiful years. And let them gather all the food of those good years that are coming, and store up grain under the authority of Pharaoh, and let them keep food in the cities. Then that food shall be as a reserve for the land for the seven years of famine which shall be in the land of Egypt, that the land may not perish during the famine* (Genesis 41:33-36).

> *Pharaoh then acknowledged before his servants, "Can we find such a one as this, a man in whom is the Spirit of God?" He continued by saying to Joseph, "Inasmuch as God has shown you all this, there is no one as discerning and wise as you"* (Genesis 41:38-39).

The key to knowing how to deliver an interpretation (and indeed how to interpret the dreams we are given) is to have a receptive heart toward the Holy Spirit. Notice that Joseph no longer is clamoring to be released. He has now dealt with the past, is filled with the Spirit of God, and is, therefore, at peace with God and with himself. This also illustrates the truth that we cannot interpret at our best when we are not in the Spirit because of overwork or stress.

SEQUENCE

Closely related to the last two major points is the importance of the sequence or order of the dream. We not only need to get the context and the overview; we also need an accurate sequence or order. Sequence relates strongly to seeing through the scenes in the dream. If, for some reason, the person who has had the dream has recorded information out of order, it can throw the intended meaning into disarray. Make sure things happened in the order they are described by listing the main points of the dream before writing up the final draft of the summary.

PAST, PRESENT, AND FUTURE

Not all dreams relate to the future. At times, God will pick a scene from the past to set the context and build faith by revealing something only you and He know, then show where you are today before moving on to where He is directing you in the future. In these dreams, the opening scene may hint of a journey. These types of dreams are relatively long and may begin in, or center on, a vessel or vehicle or a hallway or corridor.

Very often dreams reveal the state of the local church or people's hearts. These dreams are those where God discerns and discloses truth that only He and those concerned know. In disclosing this insight, He is bringing that which is not conscious to the fore so that the individual, church, or ministry can see and address issues. When these dreams are experienced by a third party, the dreamer needs tremendous wisdom and an awareness of the timing of God to know if and when he or she is to deliver the dream or its interpretation to those whom it concerns.

Are you prepared and ready to accept the responsibility of interpreting others' dreams?

_____

_____

_____

_____

_____

_____

What is your greatest joy regarding this calling? Your greatest fear?

_____

_____

_____

_____

_____

_____

_____

_____

_____

_____

_____

Not all dreams and interpretations need to be revealed. At times, some dreams are just informing you how something looks spiritually or what is happening spiritually in a situation. At other times, they are a call to prayer.

RECURRING DREAMS

When God repeats a matter, it is a sign of confirmation, importance, imminence, or urgency. A recurring dream says you weren't listening the first time. If we experience recurring dreams, we need to take note because God wants us to act on the message. When addressing Pharaoh, Joseph said, *"And the dream was repeated to Pharaoh twice because the thing is established by God, and God will shortly bring it to pass"* (Gen. 41:32).

Here Joseph explains that the recurring dream confirmed that God was speaking to Pharaoh and that what was revealed was about to happen. In Pharaoh's case, the two dreams were not identical, but they were two powerful views of the same impending issue (see Gen. 41:17-25). In the original manuscripts of the Book of John, Jesus sometimes began by saying, "Truly, truly" (John 1:51, among other occurrences). Each time, Jesus firmly captured His disciples' attention before imparting powerful spiritual truth. In much the same way today, the Holy Spirit attempts to gain our attention and impart spiritual truth through a recurring dream.

Have you received the same dream over and over? Have you discovered its meaning?

_____

_____

_____

_____

_____

_____

_____

_____

_____

When Abraham was about to sacrifice his own son in obedience to God, God caught his attention by repeating his name (see Gen. 22:11). Abraham was so intent on obedience that God had to repeat his name to break that focus and prevent the sacrifice. Likewise, today, God will break a wrong or intense focus and also impart urgency through a recurring dream.

God, in His grace, many times gives unbelievers recurring dreams concerning their eternal spiritual welfare. Dreams of people falling, washing, toileting, flying in fear, or of dark figures around the bed are strong calls for people to get things right with God so that their spiritual person has an eternal future in God's presence.

FEELINGS

The feelings of the dreamer are indicative of much of the meaning conveyed in the scenes of a dream. Even when the visual elements of two dreams are the same, the feelings of the dreamers may be vastly different. It is therefore important, where possible, to describe the feelings associated with a given situation. Anger, fear, confidence, or anxiety in a particular scene conveys just as much meaning as the visual images.

For example, flying in a dream can be either an exhilarating or terrifying experience. Both scenes describe life in the Spirit. The one accompanied by exhilaration generally conveys that the dreamer is moving in the gifts of, or flowing with, the Spirit of God. The scene that is accompanied by fear says that something is wrong spiritually: either the dreamer is not prepared for eternity (could be that he is unsaved), or he currently lacks confidence to move in the Spirit.

GENDER

When we see someone in a dream as a male or a female, it is no assurance that the person portrays someone of that gender in real life. In many aspects of heavenly thinking, both male and female are interrelated as humankind. Speaking to wives, Peter says:

> *Likewise, ye wives, be in subjection to your own husbands; that, if any obey not the word, they also may without the word be won by the conversation of the wives; while they behold your chaste conversation coupled with fear. Whose adorning let it not be that outward adorning of plaiting the hair, and of wearing of gold, or of putting on of apparel; but let it be the hidden man of the heart, in that which is not corruptible, even the ornament of a meek and quiet spirit, which is in the sight of God of great price* (1 Peter 3:1-4 KJV).

Peter, in addressing wives, speaks of them adorning the "hidden man of the heart." This nongendered aspect is also evidence that both male and female are included in Scriptures that talk about the "man of the flesh." Paul states to the Romans:

> *For we know that our old self was crucified with Him [Jesus] so that the body ruled by sin might be done away with, that we should no longer be slaves to sin* (Romans 6:6 NIV).

Both male and female are included in this call to live as though dead to sin. In other Bible versions, the "old self" is referred to as the "old man." For this reason, an old man in a female's dream can represent her "man of the flesh," that is, that aspect of her that is opposed to the Spirit.

Is gender important to your sense of identity? Why?

....

....

....

....

....

....

....

It should be noted that the man of Macedonia who appeared to Paul in a vision of the night beckoning him to come to Europe (see Acts 16:9-10) turned out to be a woman (see Acts 16:13-15).

Alternatively, it is also worth noting that a woman in a dream may also be representative of the Church (see Eph. 5:25). Often she (the Church) may be portrayed as a person's mother, sister, or even a young girl, because these may represent aspects of her (the Church) spiritually.

NAMES

The names of places and people in dreams are very significant. Sometimes the people in dreams represent themselves, and at other times, the meaning of names is a major key to dream interpretation. Or the presence of someone you know in a dream may instead point to the person's chief characteristic or what he or she represents to you.

Once again, the key is to look at the dream as a whole before assuming that the dream literally refers to that person or the meaning of his or her name. People in dreams may represent:

- Themselves

- Their character

- Their position, role, or what they represent to the dreamer

- The organization or church they represent

- The meaning of their name

The name dictionary included in *The Divinity Code* provides more than 1,200 meanings for common place and people names. However, if you anticipate interpreting a lot of dreams, you may want to consider investing in a comprehensive book of name meanings. I chose the one I use because it was relatively economical and provides more than fifty thousand name meanings.

Search engines on the Internet are also a good resource for name definitions, but be aware that many baby name websites have links to gambling and pornography. Due to variations in the agreed etymological roots of a name, it is a good idea to look at a couple of sources before accepting a name meaning as final.

NUMBERS

Numbers always provide something of significance to a dream interpretation. The implication of numbers in a dream is best shown through an example. The following dream is particularly rich in numerical significance:

In my dream I had someone whom I loved a great deal, but I hardly ever saw him. We both had a set of numbers, and the numbers were a matching set. My numbers were six, seven, eight, and his were something that went with them, but I can't remember them. So what I was going to do was to post or display my numbers so that he would see them when he went a certain way. I was going to put them up at the corner of Reservoir Road and Smart Road at the traffic circle.

This dream refers to a marital relationship. A husband and wife are to complement one another. It appears that this couple does not spend enough time together. It also appears that God is communicating to the husband through this dream. The wife's numbers are six, seven, and eight. These particular numbers in this order are a good combination, for they indicate that she is progressing spiritually. They say that she was in the flesh (six), is moving to divine perfection (seven), and is ready for a new beginning (eight) spiritually. What they spell out is a code for the husband to decipher.

> **What is the difference between determining numbers in dreams and "numerology"?**

It is possible that the husband's numbers are four, three, and two, which would be the complementary numbers to complete the order or round to ten? This combination, in this context, would mean that he now has rule (four) and will experience resurrection (three) through her unity (two) in the home. The corner of Reservoir Road and Smart Road is also significant because it says shortly (corner) she will get to the wisdom (smart) of God (reservoir) and turn around (roundabout).

This is an absolute gem of a dream. Not only does it beautifully demonstrate the potential significance of numbers in a dream, but it also ingeniously employs road names as well.

The metaphor dictionary also shows that a number may signify its face value. For example, a three in a dream may mean exactly that. As you look at the interpretation of individual elements, be sensitive to the inner voice of the Holy Spirit while you consider which interpretation for a number is the correct one. When you have the right interpretation, there will be an inner knowing or confirmatory "witness," and the message of the dream as a whole will be made apparent.

LOCAL, NATIONAL, AND CULTURAL IDIOSYNCRASIES

The dictionary of metaphors in *The Divinity Code* is based on a generally Western outlook. At times this will not be able to convey local community knowledge or the cultural perspective of a given situation.

For example, I was talking to co-author Adam one day when he instantly received a vision of a bunch of bananas being cut in half while they were being held in someone's hand. That may not mean much to you unless you know that at the time of the vision, the northern parts of Australia (the country in which we both live) had recently experienced a cyclone that decimated the banana growing regions. This meant that bananas now sold for up to fifteen dollars a kilogram, which is very expensive in our part of the country. Therefore, the vision said that something of value is going to be cut in a certain ministry situation relating to me.

How exposed are you to a larger environment on a regular basis? Do your dreams seem to change according to your sleep location?

_____

_____

_____

_____

_____

_____

_____

When you find something not mentioned in the dictionary, or a listing that does not convey your understanding of a subject, look up any relevant Bible verses relating to that subject and also write down the alternatives of what that person, place, or thing could mean to you and see which interpretation best fits the overall message conveyed in the dream.

Also realize that at times, God will stretch your spiritual understanding through the dreams He gives you. You will not always get an instant interpretation. In fact, you may have to wait days, weeks, or months before you fully understand what it was He was saying, but when the fulfillment comes, you can be sure your faith will be lifted.

PRACTICAL ADVICE

If you are going to take dreams and their interpretation seriously, it is wise to establish a dream log or journal—a notebook in which to write and date each dream you have. Leave space on the same page for its interpretation.

It is best to keep a notepad by your bed and write a few salient points, just enough to refresh your memory when you are fully awake. (If you choose to follow this technique, make sure you test your pen before turning off the light and laying your head on the pillow. There is nothing worse than waking up to find that what you thought you wrote is not on the page because the pen wasn't working.)

In the morning, arrange the dream into bullet points to maintain the correct order of events. When satisfied that you have extracted all the details, write out the dream fully in your dream journal notebook. That way you will have a permanent record of what God has been speaking to you about over a period of time.

Reading through your dreams is a faith-building exercise; you can see the things God has completed or confirmed in the past and at the same time look to where He is directing you in the future. A dream journal also provides you with things to pray about; and in praying through it, you can confidently bring Heaven to earth (see Matt. 6:10).

INTERPRETATION GUIDELINES

- Recognize that God uses dreams as a vital means of communication.

- Write the dream out immediately upon waking.

- Record any feelings associated with the dream.

- Ask God to help you both recall and interpret the dream.

- Put the dream into its correct sequence.

- Note any Scriptures that come to mind.

- Write out any "instant" thoughts about the meaning of the dream's elements.

- Utilize the metaphor dictionary for interpreting individual elements of the dream.

- Allow the Holy Spirit to piece the message together.

- Identify the subject of the dream by considering the feelings and action in the dream.

- Ask yourself, *Where in my life do I feel this way?*

- Ask yourself, *What are the current concerns of my heart?*

- Identify the theme or overall purpose of the dream by looking at it as a whole.

- Ask yourself, *Does the dream deal with the past, the present, or the future—or all three?*

- If there are hidden elements not yet revealed, hold off on the interpretation.

- Once you have an interpretation, "judge" the interpretation against the questions listed earlier.

- If you can positively identify the dream's message, move on it.

- If the dream is actually about another person, begin praying for the person.

- Thank God for His care and concern for you.

Summary

- There is no formula for interpreting dreams. It is more about cultivating a relationship with the Holy Spirit. He is the Author and Interpreter of dreams.

- Understanding comes when a person is "understanding" (or under the authority of) the Word of God. Therefore, interpretation is dependent on obedience.

- Use every opportunity to pray in tongues, particularly while traveling, as it is the vehicle for revelation, teaching, and prophecy.

- As the majority of dreams are metaphorical in nature, do not disregard a dream because it contains "weird" or recently experienced events in your life.

- Catastrophic dreams are most likely to convey a spiritual parallel.

- Dreams need to be interpreted in context. This refers not only to interpreting elements against other elements in the same dream; it also means knowing what is going on in your life—or in the life of the dreamer.

- Take your time interpreting, particularly with long dreams, because:

- You need to see the larger picture God is conveying.

- You need to confirm your interpretation of the individual elements by ensuring the whole dream makes sense.

- It takes time to see past the individual scenes to the overall message being conveyed.

- Wisdom is needed in knowing how to deliver the interpretation.

- Not all dreams relate a future scene. They may show the past, the present, the future, or all three.

- Not all dreams need to be revealed to the parties concerned. At times, some dreams are just informing us how something looks spiritually or what is going on spiritually. At other times, they are a call to prayer.

- Recurring dreams are a sign of importance, confirmation, imminence, or urgency. They indicate we weren't listening the first time.

- Many times God, in His grace, repeats dreams to unbelievers concerning their eternal spiritual destinies. Falling, washing, flying in fear, and dark figures around the bed are all calls to get right with God.

- Feelings can convey much of the meaning of a dream. Similar scenes can generate vastly different interpretations depending on the feelings experienced by the dreamer.

- Gender is not fixed in dreams. A woman may be representative of a man and vice versa. Very often the meaning of the names of people in a dream will assist in crossing this divide.

- Name meanings of people and places are very significant in dreams.

- People in dreams may represent:
  - Themselves
  - Their character
  - Their position, role, or what they represent to the dreamer
  - The organization or church they represent
  - The meaning of their name

- Numbers always are significant to the interpretation of dreams and visions.

- There will be times when the metaphor dictionary does not provide a relevant local or national cultural understanding of a particular dream or vision element. If a new understanding for a particular element fits in the overall context of the dream or vision, then feel free to use it.

- Dream and vision interpretation is a God-given gift in which a person can grow.

- Spiritual senses are developed as they are exercised.

- Each element in a metaphoric dream is like a dot in a dot painting that, once joined, becomes a story we are not likely to forget.

- The Holy Spirit will witness within our hearts about the suitability and correctness of each element of the dream—and the Holy Spirit will piece them together.

- About ninety percent of dreams are about the dreamer.

- Dreams most often address the concerns that are weighing heavily upon the dreamer's heart.

- Asking ourselves where we are experiencing the emotions and actions similar to those portrayed in a dream is a good indicator of a dream's subject.

- Every dream has a purpose.

- God will often give dreams to people in ministry that are about the spiritual well-being of those to whom they are accountable.

- When experiencing difficulty interpreting a dream, write down the dream in sequence using dot points.

- When approaching God for an interpretation, be sure to put your heart in neutral. The Bible warns about coming to God for guidance with idols (preconceived preferences) in our hearts.

- Dreams and visions show potential outcomes—either good or bad—but the outcomes are not a done deal.

- God shows problems, risks, and hazards so that we take steps to put things right before they go awry.

- Do not use a dream or vision interpretation as an excuse to act and live contrary to the Word of God.

- As dreams and visions constitute prophetic ministry, the interpretation needs to be judged according to the Scripture.

PRAYER

Father, open the eyes of my heart to see You in new and wonderful ways. I pray for a fresh revelation of Jesus. I pray for the ability to see You as I read Scripture, as I relate to others, as I wake, and as I sleep. I ask for the mantle of Joseph to be placed on me. Give me the anointing of dreamer, Lord. Help me to bring the Kingdom of Heaven to earth by delivering Your desires through dreams, revelations, visions, and words of knowledge. I pray that You would seal in my heart the things that I have learned in this course and that, ultimately, I would glorify You. In Jesus' name, amen!

SESSION EIGHT REVIEW

1. What is the only evidence of God on earth?

   A. Archeological remains

   B. Writings of Church history

   C. The Holy Spirit

   D. All of the above

2. ☐ TRUE or ☐ FALSE: The Holy Spirit uses images fresh in our memories to convey truth.

3. ☐ TRUE or ☐ FALSE: The majority of dreams come as similes.

4. God is waiting for the Church to _____.

   A. invite Him into its midst

   B. reawaken spiritual sensitivity

   C. accept dreams as communication from God

   D. all of the above

5. ☐ TRUE or ☐ FALSE: If you have a gift of the prophetic but don't know the Father's heart, that gift can become a curse.

6. The nature of Spirit-led dream interpretation is _____.

   A. redemptive and life giving

   B. edifying, not embarrassing

   C. always glorifying Jesus

   D. all of the above

7. In dreams, a wildfire is likely to indicate _____.

   A. death

   B. judgment or anger

   C. prophetic gifts

   D. creation

8. What should you do if a prophetic word or dream interpretation doesn't sit well with you?

Personal Application

Read *Matthew 1 and 2*. Notice how many times the Lord spoke through dreams at the start of Jesus' life on earth.

Continue to record your dreams in your dream journal.

You have received the training you need to begin to minister to others in the realm of dream interpretation. It's time to step out in the prophetic and put your training into action. Pray that the Lord will orchestrate divine appointments for you to meet people who mention their dreams to you. Recognize the opportunity and offer to help these people discover what the Holy Spirit is saying to them.

Review the verses you have memorized in the previous sessions.

Reading and Response

Finish reading *The Divinity Code to Understanding Your Dreams and Visions* by Adam Thompson and Adrian Beale. What impacted you most from this book during the course?

DREAM NOTES

ANSWER KEY

Session One

1. False
2. D
3. B
4. True
5. D
6. A
7. D
8. False
9. True
10. A puzzle, riddle, or parable. Answers will vary.

Session Two

1. False
2. True
3. A
4. D

5. D

6. True

7. False

8. D

9. Prayer, search the Bible, find the context.

Session Three

1. False

2. D

3. D

4. True

5. True

6. False

7. D

8. D

9. D

10. Answers will vary.

Session Four

1. B

2. D

3. A

4. True

5. D

6. B

7. False

8. False

9. D

10. God may be using the name, role, character or personality of that person to speak to you about your own heart or situation.

Session Five

1. False

2. C

3. True

4. D

5. A

6. True

7. B

8. True

9. False

10. Images help us remember; mysteries cause us to lean in to the Father for understanding.

Session Six

1. D

2. True

3. B

4. False

5. C

6. True

7. D

8. D

9. Answers will vary

Session Seven

1. C

2. D

3. B

4. True

5. False

6. A

7. True

8. A

9. False

10. We are not to put too much emphasis on dreams and visions; they are just the means to help us complete our commission to share the Gospel of salvation to others.

Session Eight

1. C
2. True
3. False
4. D
5. True
6. D
7. C
8. Put it on the shelf until confirmed by two or three witnesses.

ABOUT THE AUTHORS

ADAM F. THOMPSON has a remarkable grace to interpret dreams, move in the Word of knowledge and demonstrate the prophetic. Supernatural signs and manifestations regularly accompany his ministry as he desires to see Jesus 'magnified' through the moving of the Holy Spirit. He has ministered extensively in North America, New Zealand, Korea, and Australia. He also has spent the last fifteen years doing mission work throughout Pakistan, India, Africa, South Korea, Indonesia, Papua New Guinea, Malaysia, and the Philippines in crusades, feeding programs, and pastors conferences. Adam is instrumental in planting Field Of Dreams Church in South Australia and is the author of the *The Supernatural Man* and co-author of the bestselling book *The Divinity Code to Understanding Your Dreams and Visions* and operates itinerantly through his ministry, Voice of Fire: www.voiceoffireministries.org.

ADRIAN BEALE is an itinerant prophetic revelator who imparts the spirits of wisdom and understanding (see Isa. 11:2). His ability to see beyond the surface narratives in Scripture to reveal eternal truths is exceptional. He is co-author of *The Divinity Code to Understanding Your Dreams and Visions*, author of *The Lost Kingdom* and *The Mystic Awakening*, and loves to interpret dreams publicly and release people into Kingdom realities.

FREE E-BOOKS?
YES, PLEASE!

Get **FREE** and deeply-discounted **Christian books** for your **e-reader** delivered to your inbox **every week!**

IT'S SIMPLE!

VISIT lovetoreadclub.com

SUBSCRIBE by entering your email address

RECEIVE free and discounted e-book offers and inspiring articles delivered to your inbox every week!

Unsubscribe at any time.

SUBSCRIBE NOW!

LOVE TO READ CLUB

visit **LOVETOREADCLUB.COM** ▶

Made in United States
Orlando, FL
02 July 2024